Going Gradeless, Grades 6–12

Going Gradeless, Grades 6–12

Shifting the Focus to Student Learning

Elise Burns
David Frangiosa

Foreword by Jon Bergmann

FOR INFORMATION:

Corwin

A SAGE Company

2455 Teller Road

Thousand Oaks, California 91320

(800) 233-9936

www.corwin.com

SAGE Publications Ltd.

1 Oliver's Yard

55 City Road

London EC1Y 1SP

United Kingdom

SAGE Publications India Pvt. Ltd.

B 1/I 1 Mohan Cooperative Industrial Area

Mathura Road, New Delhi 110 044

India

SAGE Publications Asia-Pacific Pte. Ltd.

18 Cross Street #10-10/11/12

China Square Central

Singapore 048423

Publisher: Jessica Allan

Senior Content
    Development Editor: Lucas Schleicher

Associate Content
    Development Editor: Mia Rodriguez

Production Editor: Gagan Mahindra

Copy Editor: QuADS Prepress Pvt Ltd.

Typesetter: C&M Digitals (P) Ltd.

Proofreader: Eleni Maria Georgiou

Indexer: Integra

Cover Designer: Scott Van Atta

Graphic Designer: Scott Van Atta

Marketing Manager: Olivia Bartlett

Library of Congress Cataloging-in-Publication Data

Names: Burns, Elise (Elise B.), author. | Frangiosa, David (David K.), author.

Title: Going gradeless, grades 6-12 : shifting the focus to student learning / Elise Burns, David Frangiosa.

Description: Thousand Oaks, California : Corwin, [2021] | Includes bibliographical references and index. |

Identifiers: LCCN 2020048393 | ISBN 9781071837542 (paperback) | ISBN 9781071837535 (epub) | ISBN 9781071837528 (epub) | ISBN 9781071837511 (pdf)

Subjects: LCSH: Grading and marking (Students)—United States. | Educational tests and measurements—United States. | Educational evaluation—United States.

Classification: LCC LB3060.37 .B87 2021 | DDC 371.260973—dc23

LC record available at https://lccn.loc.gov/2020048393

This book is printed on acid-free paper.

SUSTAINABLE
FORESTRY
INITIATIVE

Certified Chain of Custody
Promoting Sustainable Forestry
www.sfiprogram.org
SFI-01268

21 22 23 24 25 10 9 8 7 6 5 4 3 2 1

Contents

Foreword

· ·

When I started out my teaching career in 1982, I taught tradition-ally. I lectured and hoped that students would take detailed notes. But what I thought were scintillating lectures didn't always result in deep student learning. And with my traditional teaching style, I graded everything and assigned points to every assignment. I then reported students' grades to the tenth of a percent. I did this because it was how I was taught to grade and how I was taught to teach. This practice persisted for 18 years. At first, I wasn't troubled by my grading practices, but as the years went by, I began to see the harm they did to students. My students felt an inordinate pressure to "earn points" in what really was an arbitrary system. I didn't know how to change, so I kept on doing the same things in the same way. As I look back on those first 18 years of teaching, I cringe at some of the systems I had in place.

Then, in 2007, things changed when I helped pioneer the Flipped Learning model. Instead of focusing on my teaching, I began to focus on student learning. Instead of focusing on information delivery, I began to see each student as unique and in need of their own path to optimal learning. I realized that if students didn't learn something, it was on me to make sure they understood. But in the midst of this transformation, I still clung to traditional grading.

As I began to work alongside my students more, I realized that I could take Flipped Learning to the next level. I co-developed the Flipped-Mastery model. In that model, students have to master content before moving on, which required new ways of assessment. I began to have a lot of micro-conversations with students where I formatively assessed their learning. It was during those conversations that I began to re-think what assessment should look like. I realized that the traditional grading system, where some arbitrary number determined a student's understanding, was woefully inadequate. It often measures compliance instead of real learning.

I limped along, trying to develop a grading system that actually measured learning while working within my school's commitment to the A-F grading system. I couldn't find or come up with a system that really worked. And then a couple of years ago I had a chance to talk with Elise Burns, and every bell in my brain fired all at once. After that call, I turned to a friend and said, "They have cracked the grading code."

They had developed a system that truly measures learning while at the same time taking the pressure off of students to earn points. And when I found that Elise had partnered with David Frangiosa to write this book, I was thrilled. What a book you are holding! It will not only change the way you think about grading, but more importantly, about learning. It provides super-practical guidelines to help you make the switch from earning points to assessing real learning.

The title may make it seem like Elise and David don't assess, but that isn't true. They have created a system where assessment is about learning and not about jumping through hoops to earn a grade. Their system will revolutionize your classroom and chart you onto a path that gets to the heart of what real learning is.

Jon Bergmann, High School Science Teacher and author of ten books about Flipped Learning, Including the bestseller "Flip Your Classroom," Houston, Texas.

Preface

Our goal, like that of most teachers, has been to provide our students with skills and knowledge to successfully navigate the world outside of the school building. Prior to 2015 we had each enthusiastically embraced meaningful changes in the classroom, always willing to try new strategies for the benefit of our students. We met with varying degrees of success, adding plenty of good pedagogy and methodology to our teaching toolkits. However, no one thing seemed to have the impact on student growth that we desired. After a good deal of research, as well as trial and error, we decided to go *gradeless*. This is not a pedagogical approach, or a fad, or a silver bullet. As you will find out, it is simply a frame in which any and all teaching can occur regardless of subject matter or grade level. The power of going gradeless is that you can use all of the great strategies, techniques, and approaches that work for you, but with the ability to reach even more students than ever before.

Our initial intention was simply to make our classrooms the setting for the absolute best learning experiences. As we collected data to help us improve our system, we saw the positive impact this model had, not only on our students but also on ourselves. While we didn't start out to write a book, this seemed too important not to share. We feel that our perspective as classroom teachers can help people avoid some of the growing pains that we experienced on this journey. Anyone who is either contemplating changing to or currently using a gradeless classroom can benefit from the examples we provide and discussions we have throughout the book. We will discuss in detail the *hows* and *whys* behind the decisions we made, provide concrete examples, and give you a detailed checklist to outline our pathway to going gradeless. These ideas are rooted in educational research and supported by our classroom data. We hope you benefit as much from reading this as we did while developing the system and writing this book.

Acknowledgments

··

This book would not have been possible without the overwhelming support of the Pascack Valley Regional High School District. We would like to specifically thank our students: without your open-mindedness and commitment to learning, this journey would have not have been the positive, career-changing experience it has become.

Superintendent Dr. Erik Gundersen, thank you for allowing us to take professional risks and do what we felt was in the best interests of our students.

Assistant Superintendent Dr. Barry Bachenheimer, without the opportunities you have provided us to research, present, and refine our ideas, none of this could have been accomplished.

Supervisor of Instruction Dr. Aarti Mallya, our sounding board and beacon of positivity, thank you for all the encouragement, especially through the challenging times.

Dr. Helen Friedland, thank you for giving us feedback on our earlier drafts.

And last, but certainly not least, we would like to thank our families for allowing us to dedicate time to this project and for listening to way more about assessment than I'm sure most of them would have wanted to.

Emily, thank you for lending us samples of your schoolwork and for patiently listening to the teacher's point of view. Rick, thanks for your love, support, and understanding throughout this process. And to my mother, thank you for shaping the educator I have become through our countless conversations.

Grace, thank you for your patience, support, and feedback. Charleigh and Marco, thank you for understanding when Dad was in "the work chair."

Publisher's Acknowledgments

Corwin gratefully acknowledges the contributions of the following reviewers:

Gayla LeMay
Teacher
Waycross Middle School
Waycross, GA

Michelle Strom
Middle School ELA Teacher
Fremont County Schools
Lander, WY

About the Authors

Elise Burns has been a science teacher for 30 years, teaching physics, chemistry, biology, math, and earth science. Her work is characterized by trying out new technology and approaches to provide the best possible learning experience for kids. She has presented at conferences annually at the National Science Teaching Association, Association for Supervision and Curriculum Development, or New Jersey Science Teachers Association, with workshops on rubric design, inquiry, standards-based learning, project-based learning, writing clinical evaluation reports, and assessment design, among others.

David Frangiosa has spent 14 years as a high school science teacher, teaching biology, chemistry, physics, and a number of science electives. Over that period he has been a driving force in many initiatives across multiple districts. He developed, wrote curriculum for, and taught two courses for a medical academy. As part of this initiative high school students were placed in allied health internships at a local hospital. This program piloted a paperless classroom, which led to a districtwide one-to-one program. Shortly after moving on to Pascack

Valley Regional High School District, he began conducting action research on grade reform. As a result of this work, he was asked to be on a countywide Growth Learning Assessment and Mindset (GLAM) committee. In addition to presenting these ideas within the district and at the GLAM committee meetings, he has presented at ECET2Metro, the New Jersey Science Teachers Convention, and many online workshops.

Why?

Frustration. That's how it started. I was frustrated that I had to justify every point that was deducted from an assessment. I was frustrated that I had to continuously explain to students that, no, an average of 89 at the end of the year is not just 1 point away from an A–. I was frustrated that students would try to figure out exactly what was going to be on the test. I was frustrated that students would avoid tests and quizzes, asking for extensions in an effort to gain an advantage over their classmates. I was frustrated with the constant requests for extra credit. I was frustrated with parent meetings that ended with both students and their parents in agreement that, even though learning would be nice, the only thing that colleges care about is the grade. While college admissions are clearly a valid concern, this laser focus on grade point average is a distracting obsession. True learning was my goal and could be achieved concurrently with high scores, but students needed to try a new approach. (As you will see later in this book, course averages have indeed increased since this transition.) When I continued to observe that students weren't learning, thinking, taking risks, and growing, that was my final straw. At the time I wasn't sure what was going to help them succeed in doing all of those things, but I did identify one of the major obstacles standing in their way—the unrelenting focus on grades. Instead of taking my feedback in order to improve, they were only interested in the grade itself. You have experienced this: you spend hours developing an assignment (with their interests in mind) only to have their questions about the project focus on how to get it done as fast as possible. They want to know how to get an A, while limiting their engagement to simply completing a checklist. When walking into the classroom at the beginning of the year, most students set themselves a daunting and unrealistic expectation: they need to get an A on every assignment, in every class, or the year will be a complete failure. This approach paralyzes them, preventing them from truly growing and learning! My answer to all of this is what is referred to by many as "going gradeless."

"Gradeless" does not mean that students are not assessed. It does not mean that they aren't held accountable. It doesn't mean that there aren't consequences for poor achievement. What it does mean is that they can take academic risks. The main goal of a gradeless classroom is to provide a learning environment that allows students to grow as learners without the constant fear of a single assignment having a devastating impact on their grade. The course remains rigorous. Expectations and procedures may be no different from those of a traditional classroom. However, a framework is created that makes explicit everything students are expected to know *and* do. Removing the grade also requires students to focus on the feedback, as they can no longer judge their achievement based solely on a number or letter grade.

Although the main focus of this transition is student achievement, it has also helped us, as teachers, gain a better understanding of what, how, and when to assess. Through this process, we have evaluated and restructured our curriculum to support the expected learning progression of students. Our assessments have become more focused, uniform, and relevant, which has led to consistency in the feedback provided by an individual teacher and across different teachers.

How This Book Is Organized

In the pages that follow, I am joined by my colleague and coauthor Elise Burns, with whom I have collaborated on this particular endeavor since 2016. We will take you through the reasons for our shift with a discussion of the impact of equitable grading practices (Chapter 2) and the educational theory (Chapter 3) that grounds our model. We will detail the development of our approach (Chapter 4), highlighting why certain decisions were made. In Chapter 5 we will show you how we create the learning language for each learning progression, as well as present examples from various content areas. This will be followed by how we repurpose assignments and assessments (Chapter 6). Like the majority of teachers, we are required to report a letter or number grade at the end of term, so the grade translation issue is addressed in Chapter 7. We will present the evidence, collected from five years of action research, that guided our thinking in Chapter 8 and detail a step-by-step checklist for teachers looking to transform their classroom in Chapter 9. Feel free to skip around to get your questions answered or to jump in to get started with your own development model.

A Note on Terminology

We just want to clarify some of the language used throughout the book, to avoid misunderstandings without needing to provide overly complicated explanations for each instance.

- **Striving students:** Students who are actively engaging with course content but not meeting with success—often described as "struggling" or "low achieving." We avoid these derogatory terms because they don't reflect a student's potential to succeed.

- **Feedback:** Specific, descriptive commentary (oral or written) provided to help students grow and improve.

- **Coaching, training, teaching:** These words are used interchangeably to refer to how we use feedback to move students in discrete steps in order to improve one level of development.

- **Parent:** The person responsible for overseeing the educational progress of the student we are coaching. We acknowledge that this person may not be a birth parent and may be a guardian, but for simplicity, we will generalize.

- **Child:** Again for simplicity, even though I generally refer to 11th and 12th graders as young adults, we will call students "children" to encompass all ages.

- **Schema:** The foundational understandings on which future knowledge is built.

- **Intrinsic load:** The inherent difficulty of a task or concept, which is dependent on the audience and their individual experience.

- **Retake versus reassess:** Two different approaches to allowing students to make multiple attempts to demonstrate mastery. Retaking a test (aka redoing it) means that after you give a unit 1 test, you have the option to take a new version of the same test for a second chance to demonstrate mastery. Reassessment means that after you give a unit 1 test, students have future opportunities to be assessed on the same material in a different context. As you will see, our entire approach is founded on the idea of regular, repeated reassessment, but generally, we do not see the value of retakes.

A Discussion About Equity

In schools around the country, access to education is not equal for all students. Much of this inequality centers on race, learning ability, socioeconomic status, gender, and sexual orientation. Stakeholders in many districts are trying to create a healthier, more open system in which learners feel safe, heard, and represented. While we certainly do not have an easy answer to any of these issues, one factor contributing to and exacerbating these inequities is traditional, compliance-based grading. We will touch on some of these points as we believe that our approach can be one way to create a more welcoming, supportive, and ultimately productive environment. Going gradeless can be a practical way to create meaningful change while taking into account the student's contexts and needs. With this approach IEP (Individualized Education Program) accommodations are less visible, in turn reducing the stigma of receiving educational supports. Students are not penalized for late or incorrect work during their development, which reduces the inequity that arises between students who can and those who cannot afford tutors, or between students who don't get parental support at home and those who do. Our approach is flexible and adaptable, and with some serious thought you can address many classroom situations, from the most homogeneous to the most heterogeneous.

The issues of grading equity and racism are intractably intertwined. Although we are aware of the inequities that exist as a result of biases and racism, we are not experts in that field. As to not doing any unintended harm to those discussions, we will leave that to the experts who have the knowledge and resources to provide impactful professional development that can hopefully lead to lasting positive changes in education. If you your district is looking for this type of training, please contact the experts listed in the box on the next page.

Our focus will be specifically on how going gradeless can help our students who are traditionally seen as our highest achievers and our most striving learners. We have personally seen some significant improvement with students who have learning or social issues, and have a previously demonstrated lack of engagement or ability. In addition, there are significant benefits to the upper levels, albeit for different reasons.

Equity Consultants

GOMO Educational Services

www.gomoedservices.com

Dr. Josue Falaise, Founder and CEO

Kelly Hurst

beingblackatschool.org

kelly@beingblackatschool.org

Ken Shelton

kennethshelton.net

Leading Equity Center

www.leadingequitycenter.com

Sheldon L. Eakins, PhD, Founder

First, think about the special education population, even those students who may not be classified but are striving learners for any reason. By the time we see them in high school, the primary obstacle is often their history of academic failure and subsequent resignation regarding any possible better outcome. Do you know students like that? How many times have you said to yourself, "If only they would just try!" or "Why do they give up as soon as they hit anything even moderately difficult?"

These students have been so used to "being bad" at school that often their defense is to quit before they even try. When we take away the constant grading (aka ranking), we are able to focus instead on individual student progress. So if we can simply tell them that they are doing well and get them to engage at whatever level they are, we have succeeded! And once we have clearly identified a progression of skills and understood our values and goals as educators, we could communicate to a student, "Here is where you are now. Great job!" and continue with "Here's the *one* next thing you need to do in order to progress." Moving one rung up the ladder at a time is attainable. If you do that often enough, the student will gradually gain in confidence and improve, moving slowly but surely toward the top of the ladder. One may argue that that is what an IEP is designed to accomplish. Our contention with that is it creates a system that identifies the student as the problem that needs to be provided for or fixed. Students who are placed in this box are acutely aware of it. It affects their attitude, approach, and ultimately success in school. There is nothing wrong with any student. The system is just not designed to meet their needs. A traditional grading model is centered on high-achieving students, with a focus on giving grades to sort students. A feedback-oriented assessment model has proven benefits for striving learners (Chapter 3) while not negatively affecting high-achieving students. The other benefit of this approach is that all students can engage with the same material without designation of academic ability. It meets all students where they are and celebrates their individual progress.

If you've had a long enough career, you might have noticed a gradual but systematic lowering of standards as our classes diversify and testing requirements expand. Contrary to what you might expect, without grades we get a markedly better quality of work by the end of the year than we ever used to get using the traditional method of grading. This is even more apparent in the "lower-level" courses, where the students we teach typically do not have the mathematics skills (or the confidence) to do Physics at all. Their focus on learning, and not earning grades, encourages them to try, which is leading to improved outcomes (Chapter 8). We have observed this, and students are also reporting it in the end-of-course survey.

It was the only class I actually enjoyed learning in and didn't just want to chillax and mingle with peers, like I actually enjoyed learning. Plus the system is great for kids who weren't super groomed in school.

Overall I find this class to work better for me than the usual system in all my other classes.

I enjoyed this class and the grading system. There was a lot less stress to get things done extremely fast, which allowed me to relax and learn a lot.

I found this class to be different from the rest because it wasn't as much stress to get that grade and it was more of a let's improve on what you did wrong, and I really liked that.

How does this apply to the gifted student? We often lock academically talented students into a box of striving for grades that gives them no freedom to actually think. Our best students will usually do anything you tell them to do in class, but give them an open-ended task and they are lost. Why, if they are so intelligent, do they have such anxiety? This is an issue we could explore for pages and pages, but let's just say that creativity has been trained out of them, so all they do is complete assignments without much independent thought; our Honors and Advanced Placement (AP) classes are packed with compliant students whom we love and reward for their excellent behavior (aka obedience). Why do we claim that this is inequitable? Because the current rampant level of anxiety is tied to self-worth and there are undue pressures on these "good" students. Are we serving them well, equipping them with the tools they need for success? If students have been taught that speed of computation, perfect recitation of facts, and following directions are the ingredients for success, then what happens when they get to a place where none of those are possible avenues of approach? Assuming that these students have ambitions to enter a professional field, can you think of a single career that wants a robot filling the seat of a creative problem solver? Doctors, lawyers, advertising executives, investment bankers, computer scientists, engineers, teachers, nurses, artists, financial advisors, car salesmen, and so on all need to be flexible thinkers, who take input and evaluate possible solutions, picking the best one for the situation at hand. At both ends of the spectrum, we don't provide the coaching and expectations for students to be creative problem solvers—whether because we think that they cannot, they will not, it's not expedient, or it's just not part of the curriculum. So either way, we are serving neither our historically highest nor our lowest achievers with the traditional approach.

According to Jo Boaler and Carol Dweck (2016), authors of *Mathematical Mindsets*, one can achieve equity in one's own classroom in several ways. There are two in particular that are relevant to our approach. By offering high-level content to all students regardless of their past, you send the message to all students that you believe in their abilities to learn and grow (and that they should too). By eliminating numerical grades until the end of the year, you do not penalize students for trying and failing. This means that students can put forth their best attempt at every moment, flounder and misstep, and reset when necessary and they will be able to do well in the end, regardless of the pace at which they get there. Because the types of assessments will shift due to your focus on skills, you can encourage students to think deeply by providing time for hands-on experiences, projects, real-life applications, and collaboration (Boaler & Dweck, 2016). The assessment questions can be more advanced since it's not going to matter if student responses are perfectly correct. You will be looking for clear demonstration of skill application. In Chapter 6 we will provide several concrete examples as well as student sample work.

We have found that the nature of the classroom changes. We can focus less on students having the right answer and look for positive attributes of their work that will lead them along the improvement progression. When a student gets stuck and is unsure where to start (a project or a question), together we can examine the rubric and say, "Look at the Beginner level. Can you do this?" Usually Beginner level is "trying," and usually they acknowledge that of course they can do that. Then can you move to the one thing you need to do in order to get to the Developing level? After that there is usually a mini checklist in the Proficient level that they can use as a support or some notes that they can open up for help. But we have to show them that they cannot fail as long as they simply try. Students with a history of failure need additional encouragement. The more I can say, "You can do this, I believe in you, and growth comes with effort and hard work," the more effort students make and hard work they do. It is our opinion that while we cannot change the world's ills single-handedly, if we can demonstrate true fairness by deeply believing in the abilities of *all* students, then that will have huge impacts in the future.

Last, we need to discuss homework. Many people have written extensively on this matter (e.g., Khan, 2020; Kohn, 2007), and it's a topic that we struggle with mightily on several levels. They posit that homework should be either completely eliminated or its nature limited to reflection and/or inquiry projects. Students do not have the same resources at home, whether material or emotional. For example, we each have a daughter. These girls have distinct advantages when working on homework because we have the time and ability to lend assistance. If we don't know something, we have the resources to figure it out, ask for help, or hire a tutor. And we are home every evening, available for support. What happens to someone whose parent doesn't get home until very late due to work, does not have the educational background themselves to help, does not have the financial resources to hire help, or cannot even put food on the table to nourish the brain and provide energy? What if the student has to work or babysit or is living in an environment in which study is impossible due to violence, cultural traditions, or other perceptions? Our gradeless approach enables us to reduce the amount of homework considerably and also to introduce choice about the type of homework required. There is no penalty for lateness or noncompletion. The consequence is inherent loss of practice and less opportunity for feedback. If a student doesn't hand something in or hands it in late, we only care because of our end goal for him or her to improve. If they don't complete it, we can't provide feedback. If it's late and we haven't graded the rest of the class's work, we accept it. But if we have graded the assignment, we simply mark it as done but give no feedback, unless the student comes to talk to us personally. No student has ever argued that it's fair for us to play catch-up when we are simply going to collect something else imminently and give more feedback on the same set of skills. And, of course, we have a conversation about the value of the practice as aligned with the student's self-stated goals. In the end, it's all about the conversation, reaching the student wherever he or she may be. This feels like true equity and a simple, consistent way to differentiate your classroom.

In my opinion the most coherent way to offer equitable education, regardless of socioeconomic background, gender, race, or age, is to create a culture in which it is safe to take risks, to be oneself, and to have honest conversations about failure and growth. Brené Brown, in her book *Daring Greatly*, says, "We won't solve the complex issues that we're facing today without creativity, innovation, and engaged learning" (p. 196). She lists "honest, constructive, and engaged feedback" as one of the essentials for healthy school cultures. Specifically,

> today's organizations are so metric-focused in their evaluation of performance that giving, receiving, and soliciting valuable

feedback ironically has become rare. It's even a rarity in schools where learning depends on feedback, which is infinitely more effective than grades scribbled on the top of a page or computer-generated, standardized test scores.

The problem is straightforward: Without feedback there can be no transformative change. When we don't talk to the people we are leading about their strengths and their opportunities for growth, they begin to question their contributions and our commitment. Disengagement follows. (p. 197)

One thing that our model allows us to do is have these conversations, over and over again. The elimination of grades is not enough. To create opportunities for growth, it is clear that the teacher must model and normalize the discomfort of learning. We need to help the learner appreciate how that is completely normal and healthy when learning is a productive struggle. We need to solicit feedback in the same way we provide feedback. This openness to criticism is hard to take, but if all we do is tell the students to change and we don't, they will rightly see us as hypocrites. We need to learn how to give feedback in a way that inspires growth and engagement; grades clearly do not. And to reduce anxiety, that ubiquitous presence for so many of our students, we need to let them know that when they are learning, it is *normal* to be uncomfortable. If they find it to be easy, then they aren't learning anything much at all!

Educational Theory That Grounds Our Model

With all of the tasks that teachers are expected to accomplish, reading educational research is usually pushed to the back burner, if it is considered at all. It wasn't until we each had years of experience that we considered it. Up to that point we relied on examples from veteran teachers as well as input from supervisors and administrators. Really, we were only hearing their interpretation of the educational research and acting on our interpretation of their interpretation of the research. When use of the model did not result in the impact that we hoped it would, we read the research for ourselves and found that our understandings were severely limited and, in some cases, wrong. We would highly recommend that everyone do the same and come to their own conclusions. In this section are several examples: actionable feedback, Benjamin Samuel Bloom's (1956) taxonomy, and cognitive load theory.

One of our district initiatives was to provide students with "actionable feedback." We were attempting to do this without much success, but we had no idea why our actions weren't working. Ruth Butler (1987) studied the effects of task-involving and ego-involving evaluation on student performance. Task-involving evaluation is where the comments are directed at ways by which the work can be improved, whereas ego-involving evaluation is a judgment on the quality of the work submitted, such as number or letter grades. It was observed that when students were provided with ego-involving evaluation, either in conjunction with or in the absence of task-involving feedback, interest was maintained by high achievers and undermined for striving learners. However, in both high achievers and striving learners, interest was maintained when the feedback was solely task involving. Similar observations were obtained by Anastasiya A. Lipnevich and Jeffrey K. Smith (2008), as well as others. This was eye-opening and became a deciding factor in our elimination of grades. This concept revealed the flaws in our earlier rubrics, which can be found in detail in Chapter 4. Figure 3.1 shows our initial, generic scoring rubric.

We were focused on the level of independence of the learner, which is an ego-involving judgment. To provide feedback to the student, we had to identify a deficit in that student, something they couldn't or didn't do. This had the unintended consequence of reducing that student's motivation. As we shifted to rubrics that centered language on the work being produced, rather than the learner, we saw an improvement

Figure 3.1 Generic rubric

I can ask insightful questions that are directly related to class content.

I can make advanced connections and provide helpful insights to classmates.	I can perform all tasks without error, but struggle to provide helpful insights.	I can perform the basic portions of the tasks but have difficulty with the more in-depth parts.	I can perform the basic portions of the tasks with assistance.	I have difficulty performing any part of the task even with assistance.	**Total points** 4 Points
4 Points	3 Points	2 Points	1 Point	0 Points	

in the interactions with students and the quality of work being produced. Figure 3.2 is a rubric from our most current iteration.

With this rubric, we can approach feedback from a strengths perspective. We make comments such as "Great! The conclusion makes a claim about the relationship between two variables. To make this conclusion even stronger, if there were some evidence that was collected from the investigation, it would really help make the case." With this approach the student is not in the spotlight. The feedback is a critique of the work, not the value or ability of the student.

Figure 3.2 Arguing claims rubric

	NOT ENOUGH EVIDENCE	BEGINNING	DEVELOPING	PROFICIENT	ADVANCED	EXPERT
Arguing a scientific claim	I do not write a conclusion.	I write a conclusion.	I make a scientific claim regarding the relationship between relevant dependent and independent variables, presenting evidence obtained from my investigations as support.	I make a scientific claim that accurately describes the relationship derived from any experimental results, presenting convincing evidence and stating a physics concept, theory, or equation as reasoning.	I effectively make a scientific claim, presenting the most convincing, valid, and reliable evidence obtained from my investigations as support and stating a relevant physics concept, theory, or equation as reasoning.	I effectively tie physics theory correctly, directly, and tightly to the most sophisticated supporting evidence available, so that my claim is clearly justified.

Once we decided to move away from grades, the question became "What is the best way to implement this model?" From the beginning of our respective careers, Bloom's (1956) taxonomy was an educational cornerstone and a useful model that described a hierarchy of thinking that seemed to move students from "lower-order thinking" to "higher-order thinking." All teachers want students to be able to apply course-specific knowledge in order to create something original (the highest level of the hierarchy). Our conflicts seemed to stem from students' disregard for content knowledge. How can students apply ideas that they simply do not know? To gain a better understanding of Bloom's taxonomy, I read the original work. Now that I have gone back to the source, I believe that it was not originally meant to be a hierarchy at all, as nowhere in the document did Bloom refer to lower-order or higher-order thinking. The work outlines a progression of thought with what educators now refer to as the lower levels being foundational. "As teachers we intend the learning experiences to change the student's behavior from a simpler type to another more complex one which in some ways at least will include the first type" (p. 16). Analyzing the verbs contained in the taxonomy, *remember, understand, apply, analyze, evaluate,* and *create,* it is difficult to understand what you don't remember. Students would find it challenging to apply concepts that they do not understand. For example, if students were asked to write a geometric proof proving that two triangles were congruent, there are many reasons why they could get the question incorrect. If they did not remember and understand what *congruent* meant, they would not even be able to interpret the question and would most likely leave the answer blank. If they didn't remember and understand the postulates and theorems, while they may attempt to address the question, there is no way they could apply the postulates to present a coherent argument. We can continue through the progression in this fashion, but we believe that this makes the point. These foundational elements are intended to be used to support progression through the taxonomy. This newfound understanding is consistent with our initial observations that led us to the framework of the model currently used, which will be discussed in detail in Chapter 4.

The other piece of research that has been instrumental in the success of this assessment model is John Sweller's cognitive load theory (1994), which we used to redesign our approach to organizing and delivering content. Cognitive load is related to the amount of total working memory that your brain can engage at one time, with a focus on reducing unproductive load through the use of worked examples, limiting split attention, and eliminating as many redundancies as possible. The load is broken down into three categories: (1) intrinsic load, (2) extraneous load, and (3) germane load. *Intrinsic load* is the inherent difficulty of the task, which changes based on the person and their level of experience. For example, tying one's shoes has very low intrinsic load for an adult who has been doing it for decades. However, for a child the task of learning to tie their shoes is challenging. To lower that intrinsic load, you can break the task down into discreet steps for the child to follow. With repetition the task becomes easier and easier for the child, thereby lowering the intrinsic load. Writing a lab report is one of the more complex tasks a student is asked to perform in our course. To reduce the intrinsic load of that task, we have broken the lab report into sections, only introducing one part at a time and allowing enough repetition to acquire the skill before moving on. Within each of the sections of the lab report we practice one piece at a time. For our conclusions we start with generating claims. We provide students an opportunity to practice this skill by themselves. Once students understand how to write a claim, we introduce the next piece, which is supporting the claim with evidence that they collected from their investigations, once again giving them time to practice these skills. Finally, we tie it all together with relevant physics theories. Once students have a firm grasp on writing conclusions, we would then follow a similar process to introduce how to analyze data. We continue to spiral through these skills, adding depth each time they are revisited. We will speak about the applications of this concept in detail throughout the book, as it is central to how we organize lessons, "time release" our expectations, and progress through the standards. *Extraneous load* refers to the manner in which the information is presented. For topics that have a high intrinsic load, the delivery of information should be direct and without many distractions to lower the extrinsic load. To make this point, let's use an example with which you may be familiar. When you are driving in an unfamiliar area seeking a specific location, you may turn the volume of your music down. This reduces the distractions so you can concentrate on finding the location. How this applies to our classrooms starts with the design of the course itself. If students have to spend their mental energy figuring out where to go in order to access an assignment, how to use the technology needed to learn a task, or what they should be doing during a lesson, there is less available working memory to actually understand the concept. In our course, each unit is approached in a systematic and repetitive way, which is presented in more detail later in the book. Every unit is organized into Big Ideas, which are the three to four major concepts that we use to organize the unit. Within these Big Ideas we follow the same progression toward understanding the content. We start with narrative representations of the phenomenon, which will build the foundational understandings. We then move to pictorial representations to help students visualize what is happening. Following that are graphical representations, where they both interpret and create graphs that represent the concept. Finally, they engage with mathematical representations of the phenomena. Each step of the way we are reinforcing the previous understandings. Aside from lowering the intrinsic load by breaking each Big Idea into manageable pieces, this systemized, repetitive approach frees them from thinking about what is next, leaving more mental bandwidth to focus on the content. In general, we want to lower both the intrinsic and the extraneous load in any educational setting in order to allow for more *germane load*. Germane load is the work the brain puts into storing the information in long-term memory. This is where the learning happens. As will be detailed in Chapter 6, we used this concept to modify lessons, assessments, and the sequence of the course. Most important, we have shifted to the concept of moving slower to go fast; that is, we allow students adequate time to develop a schema, the foundation on which further knowledge will be built, before moving to a new concept. By doing this we no longer have to continually reteach concepts that should have been acquired previously, allowing us to streamline later units.

Although there are other influences (Black & Wiliam, 2010; Frankin et al., 2016; Hattie & Timperley, 2007) on the model that we are currently implementing, feedback research, Bloom's taxonomy, and cognitive load theory are the driving forces behind the change. While each approach on its own can yield positive outcomes, it wasn't until they were combined that our model became a catalyst for student growth. As detailed throughout the book, these meaningful changes to our classroom would not have been possible without the implementation of these three impactful ideas.

Development of the Model, 2015–2020

David

I started my teaching career in the 2006–2007 school year as an alternate route teacher. My first teaching job was at a charter school in an urban setting. Reflecting on that experience, there were many mistakes made as a novice teacher without the benefit of an educational preparatory program to guide me, as well as due to the lack of perspective on the conditions necessary for students to learn. It wasn't until later in my career that I realized the inefficiencies and inequities that a traditional educational model brought with it. I made some excuses as to why students weren't learning. That first year I taught in a converted warehouse with no functional science labs and limited access to technology. I was charged with teaching biology, environmental science, and a class called "The Human Organism." In August, when I was hired, I asked for the curriculum to prepare for the upcoming school year. I was told that there was no curriculum. Figure out what I wanted to teach, find some textbooks, and give them a list of needed materials. They would see what they could get for me. Being that this was my introduction to teaching, I wasn't exactly sure what supporting teachers and students was supposed to look like, but this definitely didn't seem like it. Throughout the year I built relationships with students, and they did learn some things, but it was easy for me to rationalize their lack of success as being a product of their environment, the lack of resources, or simply their not caring. At the end of that first year I was offered an opportunity to teach in a public school. Knowing the district prior to working there, I knew that I would be provided the resources and support I thought I would need to make a positive impact. While things were better initially, I still wasn't seeing the results that I wanted. I built relationships with the students and thought that I was doing everything in my power to create a learning environment that would help them succeed. Once again, as an inexperienced teacher I chalked it up to the students not caring about their education as much as I did. Looking back, this is completely unfair. The issue at hand wasn't that students didn't care; it was the fact that our goals were not aligned. However, after spending five years in this district, the frustration got to a point that I needed to make a change. I was fortunate enough to be offered a job in one of the most well-respected districts in our area for the 2012–2013 school year. As I faced this new group of students, on the surface our goals initially seemed aligned. The students cared greatly about their grades and were compliant (my least favorite word in education). In this setting the students were very focused on earning a grade. They identified with that grade. Learning was secondary. I would ask what they had learned in a course and be met with a response like "I did pretty good. I got an A." Never answering the question of what they had actually learned. This is when I realized that what I was observing was not unique to an individual student, district, or demographic but a symptom of our educational system as a whole. When I tried many things to try to refocus on learning, I had various degrees of success, with none of them having the impact that I desired. That brings us to the 2015–2016 school year and my journey with going gradeless. As you will read, it was not a smooth transition, and there were mistakes made along the way. With all of the varied approaches to standards-based grading, we felt that it was important to highlight these and explain our reasoning for selecting certain practices while moving away from others. Even with the detours that we made as we navigated this new path, we always kept the best interests of students as the central focus. We persevered through challenges and now have a reliable, transformative model that works for students and teachers alike.

The Beginning: 2015–2016

I have always structured my course around desired outcomes. These outcomes had little to do with the course content and everything to do with lifelong skills that, in my opinion, would greatly improve the minds of the students in any arena. Although the content of a particular course is important, it is used as the vehicle for, not the goal of, learning. At the beginning of the 2015–2016 school year my students were not making significant progress toward my outcomes. As mentioned previously, my goals and those of the students were completely different: theirs was to get an A, while I wanted students to increase personal engagement, develop a desire to learn, acquire knowledge and skills, and apply their knowledge and skills to new situations. At this point I decided that something needed to change, so I began researching alternate assessment models. I didn't really know what I was looking for and had no preferred model in mind. I was hoping that I could structure an environment where students wanted to engage with the content and I could simply be a coach to guide them through the process. When I came across the idea of "I can" statements, I liked the positive message that they conveyed to students. Shifting the focus away from what students couldn't do to what they could do resonated with me. My original plan was to take the entire school year and develop "I can" statements, align them with the curriculum I was currently teaching, and prepare to use this model at the beginning of the 2016–2017 school year. I went topic by topic and developed "I can" statements for content knowledge and process skills. By November I had my entire curriculum completed—60 "I can" statements, with each

Figure 4.1 Generic rubric

I can ask insightful questions that are directly related to class content.

I can make advanced connections and provide helpful insights to classmates.	I can perform all tasks without error, but struggle to provide helpful insights.	I can perform the basic portions of the tasks but have difficulty with the more in-depth parts.	I can perform the basic portions of the tasks with assistance.	I have difficulty performing any part of the task, even with assistance.	**Total points** 4 Points
4 Points	3 Points	2 Points	1 Point	0 Points	

statement being assessed on the same, generic 0–4 scale (see Figure 4.1). My overall vision was that every interaction with a student could become an assessment. I imagined myself walking around with a clipboard continuously monitoring when students showed proficiency in any of the "I can" statements at any time.

According to the rubric, as student independence and competency improved, their score would increase. In my thinking the more independently students worked, the higher their mastery level. Every attempt at these statements would be tracked and an overall score calculated using a decaying average (see Figure 4.2). (A decaying average is a scoring system that makes the final attempt worth the highest percentage and all previous attempts are averaged together for a smaller percentage of the overall score.)

Decaying averages would allow students to practice, make mistakes, and grow slowly, all without the penalty of being dragged down by a low score that is nearly impossible to improve. At the same time they were still accountable for all their work, since all assignments were tracked

Figure 4.2 Decaying average

EXAMPLE OF A TRADITIONAL AVERAGE				
SCORE 1	**SCORE 2**	**SCORE 3**	**SCORE 4**	**AVERAGE**
60	70	80	90	75
EXAMPLE OF A DECAYING AVERAGE (FINAL 80%)				
SCORE 1	**SCORE 2**	**SCORE 3**	**SCORE 4**	**FINAL SCORE**
60	70	80	90	
Average = 70				
20% of average = 14			80% = 72	72 + 14 = 86

and did count at least a little. The final attempt, however, counted for 80% of the overall grade and would have the most impact. This means that the rate of skill acquisition would not hurt or help significantly. What mattered was that by the end of the school year, the students were performing at their best. Another related feature of the change in my approach was that students would be able to choose what they wanted to use for this final attempt: a written test, a project, or an oral exam. While they had to complete all three regardless of their choice, they could select one to count as the 80% assessment. This would allow every student to demonstrate their mastery in their most comfortable setting.

Close to midyear I became excited about the potential of this new approach and increasingly impatient and unwilling to wait for the next school year. I wanted to implement this new system at the start of the second semester. Over the next month I met with my supervisor, the building administration, and the director of curriculum to vet this approach. After much discussion, they agreed to let me try it. I wasn't sure that it was going to work, but I knew that what I was currently doing absolutely *wasn't* working. We set up a trial lesson with volunteer students. I had my "I can" statements on my clipboard, ready to track progress while interacting with students in a fully attentive manner. Within an hour I had already realized that that approach wasn't going to work. The clipboard made every interaction seem clinical and made students feel like they were under constant scrutiny, plus I couldn't both track and attend to them simultaneously. I made some necessary adjustments and decided to move forward.

The best thing I did during this transition was proactively communicate with the students and their parents. Knowing that this was a major shift for both of them, I set up parent information nights. I invited them into the classroom and explained what I was planning on doing and why I thought it was necessary. I allowed them the opportunity to question me. I answered every single question as honestly as possible. They were able to vent and accuse me of being the reason why their student wouldn't get into college, which I entertained and responded accordingly. Whatever was on their mind, I gave them the floor. By the end of those sessions, they may have disagreed with me, some vehemently, but they knew that I had the student's best interests in mind. I assured them that even though this was not going to be perfect, we would correct any unforeseen negative impacts that arose.

So when the second semester began, I went ahead without the clipboard. At this initial implementation, even with the information nights, there was a significant amount of pushback from both parents and students. Since this was not a school initiative, I was the only teacher doing this, and the idea was completely different from their past educational experience, this was pretty understandable. Most of the concerns were centered on not being able to track the grade. However, the more open-minded students soon realized that the only thing changing about the class was how their work was being reported, since the established routines and the types of assessments hadn't changed at all at this point. As the year progressed, it became clear that the previously striving students were the ones who were benefiting the most from the transition (evidence will be presented in Chapter 8). In a traditional grading model, the student who is receiving a C, D, or F perceives negative feedback; in other words, everything they do is wrong. Receiving descriptive feedback (instead of just the label) shifted the conversation to what they were doing well and how they could expand on those positive skills to improve other areas of their work. Being able to choose which format counted as their final attempt was very powerful for this specific population of students, most of whom felt that they were poor test takers. They now felt that they had a fair chance. However, this was by no means a seamless transition or a finished product. First, there were no real differences in their performance across the three types of final assessments, so any of them could have been used without changing their rating in the standards. Second, the turnaround time for feedback suffered because I had to evaluate three different end-of-unit assessments for every student. Third, the monitoring of which one counted as the final attempt for which student was a logistical challenge. Additionally, there were a significant number of students who were resistant to the feedback and never got on board. Another challenge that I encountered in that first run was communication. Our gradebook wasn't set up to deliver the type of information I was trying to provide. Nor was I very eloquent in my presentation when speaking to parents and students. Part of the reason for that was my uncertainty about what the final product was going to look like. Most significantly, I quickly realized that with 60 "I can" statements there was a lot of overlap and it was very cumbersome to manage.

So given the limited success why did I continue? I gave students a survey about their self-assessed growth in the traditional model, before implementation, in January 2016, and again in June 2016 for the feedback-based assessment model. Although the survey results were encouraging, there was one student who tipped the scales for me. In the first semester I would have to track this student down. She would ask to go to the bathroom and be gone for the majority of the period. She rarely completed any assignments and left the majority of her tests blank. There was nothing I could do to motivate her. By the end of the first semester her average was 44%. Early in the second semester, I gave an assessment using our new standards. While the majority of the assessment was evaluated at 0–1, there was one thing this student was very good at and that was evaluated at a 3. This authentic win for her changed her approach to the class. She was blown away that she had the ability to be successful in *anything* related to science. We had the conversation that there were some things that she did well and we needed to start with those areas and expand. From that point forward, she rarely left class and was a more active participant during class time. She eventually became the leader of her lab group and was completing more assignments than not. Her second semester grade was 77%. Seeing the same student behave like two entirely different people, with the only alteration being the assessment model, I knew that this is what I had to do. Even with all of the challenges that I knew were ahead of me, I was encouraged enough by the positive effects of the switch to know that I was never going back to traditional grading.

The end of the 2015–2016 school year was a very important time for me. It was at this point that one of my colleagues, Elise Burns, decided that as she had seen enough positive effects from my transition, she was going to try it as well, starting with the 2016–2017 school year. We taught the same course and shared a classroom, so I was excited to have more input from someone whom I trust and respect. That doesn't mean we always agree, but we have had excellent conversations to hash out our differences. This made the process the most efficient and productive one I have ever had the pleasure to be a part of. Even though we disagreed on how to accomplish the task, we were in complete agreement with what we were trying to accomplish. With the 2016–2017 school year, my goal was to condense my "I can" statements to the smallest number that represented all the content and skills I was trying to assess (which turned out to be 30). Elise had a more detailed list of "I can" statements. We agreed that for the first year we would do things independently and track our progress. We would talk regularly, comparing successes and failures.

So let me allow Elise to introduce herself at this point, as she will be contributing much more to the conversation from here on.

Elise

I too got into teaching via the alternate route, back in 1994. Beginning as a part-time earth science and physics teacher, I launched my career with support but little expertise. My educational background was in engineering and fine arts/art history, and I was far from the stereotypical science teacher. I used this background to my advantage, always trying to capture students by using immersive, large-scale projects and alternate viewpoints, attempting to bring their creative interests (and mine) into the science classroom. While earning my master's degree in curriculum and instruction in 1996, I learned more about rubrics and authentic assessment, and science education specifically. Over the next 10 years I became a missionary of rubrics and design projects, presenting at conferences and working with colleagues. I have always felt as if I ended up teaching physics by accident, due to demand as opposed to my own desire, and therefore never felt attached to the content itself. Yes, it was interesting, relevant, and complex, and required fun math to complete well, and I enjoyed it. Yet what I really wanted was to teach. Teaching skills that students could use regardless of the class was a passion of mine. Things like critical thinking, presentation and communication, problem solving, and design, which would improve their lives, our lives, and our country as a whole. What I quickly noticed was that no matter what district I was in, I ended up with the same struggles: a battle between authentic learning versus grade earning. I kept trying, tweaking my approaches or adopting new models like project-based learning, but saw no overall effect. The only thing I never thought of was going gradeless.

On a more personal note, over the years I watched my own daughter's growing obsession with grades, the resulting anxiety about performance, and worsening disenchantment with all of her classes. Despite being a perceptive and intelligent young person, she escaped more and more into bad academic habits and consumption of media and developed an indifference to learning. She equated her own value as a person with her performance. Part of this was her age; middle school and early high school are unkind to parents and children alike. But to see a bright, thoughtful person who has always loved learning fall into that kind of thinking even when raised by someone like me? It was hard to watch her be so heavily influenced by the culture, both online and in school. This motivated me even more to try to influence the students with whom I interacted. I wanted to create one of the few spaces in school where students could come to learn without the constant pressure of being perfect.

In 2015–2016 I was in my 21st year of teaching and listening to Dave talking about his ideas and subsequent experiences with the "I can" statements. We had the same goals, but even for a chameleon like me, it was hard to change my approach and mindset. I decided to let him experiment on his own that second semester; but once I saw the results, I jumped on the bandwagon. What I bring to our partnership is expertise in and experience with assessment, rubric creation, and curriculum design, as well as 9 million questions. After so many years of evaluating work based on percentages, accumulated points, or other value systems, I made Dave really think hard about the whys, hows, and what ifs of this approach. We hashed this out over the next several years, and my hope is that I can provide you with a straight-line path to success without all the twists and turns we ended up making.

First Revision: 2016–2017

As we prepared for that school year, we focused on communication. We wanted to send a clear message to the students and parents about what we were trying to accomplish, our philosophy behind the approach, our expectations, and what they could expect from us. We modified our gradebooks to reflect this new approach. An email was sent home detailing to parents how to interpret the information they would be receiving and how to track their children's growth. We provided another information night, in addition to the normal back-to-school night, for parents to come in and ask questions to clarify the finer points of the assessment model. Our goal was to make everything as transparent as possible. Due to this much more effective communication, the start to this school year was significantly smoother than the transition at the midyear of the previous one. In addition, we had a clearly stated purpose; a refined, systematic approach; and two implementors instead of one. Students were, of course, still concerned about their grades, but they seemed much more willing to step outside their comfort zone. While all this was positive, I still wasn't getting the academic results I was expecting. On my end, it was easy to identify the areas of strength and the areas in need of improvement. However, this communication wasn't translating to student success in any of our classes, so we knew that the message we were trying to send wasn't getting delivered. At that point we weren't sure exactly what needed to change; we just knew that something had to change.

As part of the process we would regularly do student surveys and talk to students about their experiences and thoughts of the assessment model. During these interactions the students were very honest about their views, which was extremely helpful. They let us know that the classroom culture we had developed was very successful in reducing student stress about learning. They understood that learning was a progression and they were not penalized for the results earned while they were building skills. The problem occurred because they did not feel the sense of urgency to do their best work on every assignment. They would prioritize other classes that were still using traditional grading and leave our work for last, if they got to it at all. This was contradictory to what we had anticipated. Our original plan was to present academic challenges that could be attempted without the fear of getting a bad grade. However, that was not explicitly communicated to the students, and at that point it would not have been fair to penalize students for an oversight on our part. As soon as we realized that this was an issue, we stressed the importance of continually doing their best work because when they got to the assignments that would eventually hold the most weight, they would not be prepared. Some students responded positively, while there were still too many who procrastinated. We knew that this would have to be addressed in the next version of our model. One of the other significant obstacles they were facing was that they didn't fully understand the "I can" statements or how to progress through the levels of independence. We agreed that the language and presentation of these statements needed to be refined prior to the beginning of the next school year.

We are fortunate enough to work in a district that thinks outside the box in terms of professional development, which led to opportunities for Dave to visit schools that were experimenting with competency-based learning and gradeless classrooms. The first trip was to a suburb of Chicago, where a little over 50% of classes were using a competency-based model. They were also using "I can" statements, but they had only six standards they were evaluating per course, and all of their standards were process skills. Each standard was assessed on a 4-point scale, with distinct statements about how well they performed that specific skill and whether that skill was exhibited in a familiar or an unfamiliar context. While that idea was good, the lack of content was difficult to swallow. Understanding that they were using the content as the evidence for growth, we were not comfortable not having content represented explicitly, so we decided that we would still assess content. A second trip during the 2016–2017 school year was to a high school in Connecticut that was transitioning to a competency-based diploma; those students would not see a letter or number grade for their entire public school career. This school used habits of scholarship, which were all of the behaviors that support academic success, such as punctuality, completion of assignments, participation, and so on. These did not factor into the overall assessment of the standards, but they were reported.

Armed with the information gleaned from these trips, our experience with the full year of implementation, and the results of the student surveys, we identified several areas that needed tweaking. However, we felt enthusiastic about the positive results and confident that we were heading in the right direction.

Refining and Reorganizing: 2017–2018

By this time, we had a firm grasp on what we were trying to accomplish, how we would support the pathway to attaining that goal, and how to communicate our vision. The school year started smoothly, and we had virtually no community pushback at this point. This was the result of changes in several areas and a real shift in understanding of what we could accomplish.

• *Adjusting the "I can" statements:* We grouped "I can" statements together into packages, so that we had nine content standards (instead of three to five per unit) and six process standards. This increased flexibility in our assessments because we had fewer boxes to check. We shifted the success criteria from a subjective scale of student independence to more objective statements about what students can do or should know, with each step building on the previous one. For example, Figure 4.3 provides a 4-point scale for the process standard experimental design.

Figure 4.3 Four-point scale

0: Not enough information to evaluate.

1: I use the tools and equipment effectively to collect data related to the stated task and organize them into a table.

2: I can ask a question that is directly related to the assigned task and communicate the methods and materials used during the investigation. The data are precise and complete, and can be used to answer the question.

3: I can ask testable questions that are directly related to the assigned task. I can plan and implement effective data collection strategies and communicate this clearly, succinctly, and with sufficient detail.

4: I can develop an investigation that can produce data to answer a question in an unfamiliar context.

- *Unit sequencing:* Realizing that certain skills needed to be obtained before students could progress to the next level, we rearranged the order of our units to move from simpler skills to more advanced. In Physics traditionally, the first unit of study is kinematics, or the study of motion. Not only do students need to learn new vocabulary, but there is also a huge emphasis on developing problem solving, graphing, and multifaceted lab skills. However, some units usually done later in the year, such as electric circuits or waves, have pretty basic mathematics and need purely observational lab skills. So we put the circuits unit first and began kinematics several months later, once the simpler skills were mastered. The new sequence and modified assignments provided the anticipated opportunities to build the foundational skills and progress through the standards.

- *Checkpoints:* We moved away from graded quizzes to self-assessed progress check-ins that we call checkpoints. Each week students take 15–20 minutes to answer a set of questions. Immediately after time is called, every question would be reviewed on the board, with students required to annotate their own papers with corrections. They would then evaluate their work based on the criteria in the rubric, which was printed at the top of the checkpoint. At that point the teacher provides detailed, directed feedback about the attributes and characteristics of each performance level. This has the benefit of teaching students how to read the rubric, the boundaries between levels, and what to do to reach the next level. By providing students with immediate, relevant feedback, we focus conversations on current strengths and where improvements need to be made. Contrary to what you might believe, students actually try harder on these assessments than they would have if they counted as a grade. You might think that they would blow them off since they aren't collected or recorded. However, removing the pressure caused most students to respond without worrying about "looking stupid," using all of the given time, marking up their papers during review, and asking clarifying questions. In addition, we saw reduced test avoidance and anxiety. Many students viewed this as an opportunity to simply see where they were academically, without the pressure of a grade, like a practice test.

- *Missing and incomplete work:* As detailed in Chapter 8, the survey results showed that students would deprioritize our assignments because they didn't "count." We needed to address students' lack of urgency, so we began by making unit projects mandatory. If a project was not completed, regardless of how students did on the rest of the course assignments, they would not be eligible for course credit. How we deal with missing work is described in Chapter 7.

- *End-of-unit mastery:* At the end of each unit, recall that we assigned three assessments (project, unit test, and oral presentation) that checked mastery on the same content and process skills. This was neither needed nor effective. Instead, we eliminated the oral presentation (most students hated that anyway), keeping the project to develop engineering design skills (a centerpiece of the Next Generation Science Standards [NGSS]) and the unit test for content knowledge. This streamlined the assessment process and reduced the student workload, while allowing us to provide prompt feedback and clear comprehension of student progress on the skills on which we were working.

- *Cumulative exams:* We still wanted to expose students to longer exams like midterms and finals. However, we wanted more flexibility, so we administered three cumulative exams. Instead of providing a multiple-choice assessment of content, we assessed what we called "test-taking skills," such as applying previously learned information and combining concepts in more complex ways. This was interesting and raised new concerns, to be addressed later.

- *Conferencing and portfolios:* One of the shortcomings of grading of any sort is the lack of understanding of *what the grade represents.* Whether using a traditional approach or a gradeless approach, we want students to be fully aware of what their score or grade means regarding their progress. We began individual conferencing with every student two or three times a year. The goal here was to involve students in the process and have them take ownership of their education, rather than feel like a grade was a judgment placed on them. In an effort to encourage metacognitive skill development and a conversation grounded in artifacts, we also made an electronic portfolio a requirement of the course. Students would select pieces of work that exhibited their level of mastery in the standards. They could correct the work, annotate it, or create something new on their own. Along with those artifacts students would have a journal of their progress, detailing struggles, successes, or anything else they felt was valuable to note. During these conferences students would use their portfolios to justify their level of progress in each standard. We discussed their strengths, their weaknesses, and their goals, and together we developed a learning plan to move forward. We also discussed discrepancies between their self-evaluation and our evaluation of their skills and knowledge. This was important in helping them understand how to progress through the standards. These discussions were very effective; however, they took roughly a week and a half of class time to complete, which we knew needed to be streamlined. Therefore, all conferences in the second half of the year were held outside of class time by appointment.

- *Habits of scholarship:* We also decided to create an ongoing progress report in our gradebook. Taking the idea sprouted from the school visitation the previous spring, we created our version of Habits of Scholarship that would inform students (and their parents) of the behaviors that might be impeding their academic growth.

These changes brought a lot of growth for us as educators. The effect on the teacher–student relationship was huge and had a tremendous effect on the classroom atmosphere. However, there were still some sticking points. For example, we noticed that student growth seemed to plateau after January. We did not see real increases in skill or knowledge from this point because students were rarely taking action on the feedback they were receiving. Few students came for extra help. The interdependence of process and content in the standards led to confusion and a lack of understanding of the requirements to move from one level to another. In addition, we still needed a better system of accountability—some way to get students to submit assignments regularly. There were still too many students who were not recognizing the spirit of the assessment model. They were certainly well-informed about the intent: the more work you submit, the more feedback you receive, the more improvement you make, the more growth you exhibit, and the higher your achievement will be. Regardless of how many times we said it, some students would still do the bare minimum, and therefore their comprehension would suffer. We also identified a clear need to differentiate the students who were striving to understand the content from the students who did not submit assignments at all. All of these challenges would be addressed in our next iteration of this model.

Realigning: 2018–2019

This was the most effective revision of our model: a great realignment of form and function.

- *A 5-point scale:* Our previous model did not distinguish between hard-working, striving students and students who did not complete and turn in their work. To address this, we shifted our scoring rubric from a 4-point scale to a 5-point scale for all process standard rubrics, as seen in the experimental design rubric in Figure 4.4. This enabled us to include a 0 level to distinguish students who did not turn in enough assignments from the first level, where students at least tried to meet the requirement.

  Note that levels 2–5 are essentially identical to levels 1–4 from the previous year. The change is the insertion of a level 1, which gives credit essentially for trying to submit something— anything at all.

- *Separation of content from the practices:* This was the biggest, most audacious change that we made. It was one of those things that we could not have even imagined doing a few years earlier; yet once done, it seemed completely intuitive. We significantly clarified the language in the standards to make the learning progression more clearly defined, pulling all content out of the

Figure 4.4   Five-point scale

0:	Does not complete enough assignments to assess.
1:	I collect and/or present data.
2:	I use the tools and equipment effectively to collect data related to the stated task and organize them into a table.
3:	I can restate the task as a question that is directly related to the assigned task and communicate the methods and materials used during the investigation. The data are precise and complete, and can be used to answer the question. The data table is well organized.
4:	I can ask testable questions that are directly related to the assigned task. I can plan and implement effective data collection strategies and communicate this clearly, succinctly, and with sufficient detail. The data table is well constructed, including columns for analysis relevant to the labs.
5:	I can independently develop an investigation that can produce data to answer an independently generated question.

standards so that the skills and practices could be assessed independently of the content and, most important, used across *all* units.

○   We had to make sure that when we assessed content, students were being assessed only on content and not mixing in practices, which is really the *application* of the content. Addressing the content knowledge was not difficult, but the setup was time-consuming. We had "I can" statements for the entire curriculum and organized them by topic. We asked ourselves the question "What is the absolute minimum a student would have to know or do in order for us to be comfortable saying they took my class and passed?"

❖   The answer to the "knowing" was what we later referred to as foundational concepts. Any "I can" statements that were definitions or content-specific terminology (aka the knowledge or comprehension levels of Benjamin Samuel Bloom's taxonomy) were the scaffold on which all other skills were hung. These statements became the minimum *content* necessary to receive credit in the course. Content would be assessed as Pass or Fail early in each unit, since this base knowledge is needed to progress through the process standards. How we do this is described fully in Chapter 6. Our goal is to have students become completely fluent with these definitions and understandings so that they can use them when they have to demonstrate skill mastery.

❖ The answer to the "doing" was what we called the standards or practices. Once we pulled the content out, we were left with a handful of skills that repeat across every unit and closely parallel our national science practices (NGSS). We ended up with eight standards, addressing a wide assortment of skills needed to write up a lab, solve problems, produce an engineering solution, create and interpret graphs, write scientific explanations, and use feedback.

○ This had a *huge* impact on our understanding of our courses. Once content was pulled out, we realized that we were working on the exact same skills in every physics course, no matter what level (we have five). The only differences were the level at which the students came into the course in September and the expectations for improvement over the school year. For example, you might expect an AP student to work their way up to the highest level of problem solving to get an A, but a College Preparatory (CP) student could demonstrate Proficiency or Advanced to get an A. This transformed and streamlined our rubric design and made the grade translations really clear and efficient. In addition, the basic course content is nearly identical whether you are in Conceptual Physics or AP Physics; therefore the same content mastery quizzes could be used for all classes. The only differences are the pace and the breadth of the content; AP Physics would complete more units in a year and therefore take more content mastery quizzes.

• *Presentation of levels:* Although this is seemingly minor, we made a meaningful shift in the order in which the standards were presented. We originally had presented the criteria with the ideal standard listed first. Students would have to read three statements before they would get to the criteria they needed to address first. See, for example, the original 5-point scale in Figure 4.5 for the process standard experimental design.

Our experience was that students would read the ideal standard (listed first) and try to provide evidence that they met that criteria *without addressing any of the criteria of the previous statements.* They did not understand that this was a *progression.* If they did not meet the requirements of level 1, they could never be assessed as completing any level after that. This was an easy fix. In our current model, we present the

Figure 4.5   Original 5-point scale

5:   I can independently develop an investigation that can produce data to answer an independently generated question.

4:   I can ask testable questions that are directly related to the assigned task. I can plan and implement effective data collection strategies and communicate this clearly, succinctly, and with sufficient detail. The data table is well constructed, including columns for analysis relevant to the lab.

3:   I can restate the task as a question that is directly related to the assigned task and communicate the methods and materials used during the investigation. The data are precise and complete, and can be used to answer the questions. The data table is well organized.

2:   I use the tools and equipment effectively to collect data related to the stated task and organize them into a table.

1:   I collect and/or present data.

0:   Does not complete enough assignments to assess.

Figure 4.6   Reordered 5-point scale

0:   Does not complete enough assignments to assess.

1:   I collect and/or present data.

2:   I use the tools and equipment effectively to collect data related to the stated task and organize them into a table.

3:   I can restate the task as a question that is directly related to the assigned task and communicate the methods and materials used during the investigation. The data are precise and complete, and can be used to answer the question. The data table is well organized.

4:   I can ask testable questions that are directly related to the assigned task. I can plan and implement effective data collection strategies and communicate this clearly, succinctly, and with sufficient detail. The data table is well constructed, including columns for analysis relevant to the data.

5:   I can independently develop an investigation that can produce data to answer an independently generated question.

standards with the most basic criteria first (as given in Figure 4.6 for the process standard experimental design).

When presented in this fashion, students must satisfy the first set of criteria they read before they move on to the next statement. This makes their task clearer and reinforces the concept of a progression.

- *Selection of tasks:* Similar to most teachers, we have many more assignments than we could ever complete in a given year. For each concept, there may be five different labs we could do. Instead of choosing randomly (relatively speaking), we made curricular decisions based on what we chose to emphasize. For example, some labs and projects are more optimal earlier in the year because they are more observational, with less sophisticated analysis required. Toward the second half of the year, we include the more complex ones to enable those ready to progress, grow, and improve. This complemented the change of the unit order that we had made in 2017–2018 and helped emphasize the continuity of the course as a whole.

- *Grade translation:* This is where so many of us get hung up. How do we implement a standards-based grading system within a traditional one? When working within our traditional school system, grades need to be reported at the end of the semester and the year. We came up with a simple guide that worked like the rungs in a ladder. There was no continuum but quantum divisions between grades. To accommodate varying student strengths, we simply allowed students to accumulate a specific number of practices at a particular level, with a minimum for all the remaining practices. For example, if a student had four of the nine skills at level 3, and the remaining five skills were at a minimum of level 2, they earned a B. If another student had similar scores, but even one skill at level 1, they earned a C. In other words, we created a basement for each grade: a student earned a C if some skills were still at the "trying" stage; a student earned a B if their skills had moved up to the "I'm using some physics" stage. This was published at the beginning of the year so that everyone knew the expectations and could see what achievement levels they needed to acquire in order to meet their goals. The scale was simply shifted up or down depending on the course: an Honors course would have higher benchmarks to achieve the same end-of-year grade.

- *Minimum requirements:* Although we had seen improvements in student accountability, there was still significant room for growth. We decided that we would outline our minimum requirements for credit to have students actively track their completion of the tasks. Students who completed these requirements would have provided us with enough evidence to effectively evaluate their performance. Again, we asked ourselves the question "What is the absolute minimum that a student would have to produce for me to say that they completed the course?" The minimum requirements address all of the criteria we were assessing throughout the year and were organized into a checklist (see Figure 4.7). The checklist

Figure 4.7   Minimum requirements

Lab reports

UNIT NAME	#	LAB NAME	DATE
DC Circuits	1		
	2		
Magnetism	1		
	2		
Kinematics	1		
	2		
Newton's Laws	1		
	2		
Energy	1		
	2		
Momentum	1		
	2		
2D/Circular/ Gravitation	1		
	2		

Peer reviews

UNIT NAME	#	LAB/ STUDENT NAME	DATE
DC Circuits	1		
	2		
Magnetism	1		
	2		
Kinematics	1		
	2		
Newton's Laws	1		
	2		
Energy	1		
	2		
Momentum	1		
	2		
2D/Circular/ Gravitation	1		
	2		

Content

UNIT NAME	PASSED
DC Circuits	
Magnetism	
Kinematics	
Newton's Laws	
Energy	
Impulse and Momentum	
2D/Circular/ Gravitation	

Projects

PROJECT NAME	COMPLETION DATE

Checkpoints

UNIT NAME	COMPLETION DATE
DC Circuits	
Magnetism	
Kinematics	
Newton's Laws	
Midterm	
Impulse and Momentum	
Energy	
2D/Circular/ Gravitation	
Final	

was kept in the student portfolio, and time was provided for students to update them occasionally. This does not count for a grade in and of itself; completing the minimum requirements enables a student to pass the course. Their grade is determined by the grade translation chart for that course, which will be discussed later.

- *Portfolio:* The concept of the portfolio had worked well the previous year, enabling both students and the teacher to track performance more qualitatively, but the electronic version was too cumbersome. Too much time was spent formatting and troubleshooting the portfolio itself, rather than focusing on the artifacts it contained. We reverted to a paper portfolio. The artifacts include a periodic narrative addressing the growth, challenges, accomplishments and goals, annotated lab reports, peer reviews, problem sets, and project reports. These artifacts serve as evidence for mastery of the process skills and as a great jumping-off point for conferences.

- *Weighting:* We completely eliminated the decaying average. One of the main reasons for using the decaying average was to create a system of accountability. With the minimum requirements for credit in place to keep students on track, it was no longer necessary to use the decaying average. In its place, the most recent assessment score serves as the current rating in each standard. At the end of each unit, past scores are simply replaced with the newest score, for better or for worse.

Ongoing Adjustments: 2019–2020

Heading into the next year, we were thrilled with the effectiveness of the changes listed above. Besides the evidence (see Chapter 8), it just *felt* good. We both had relationships with students that were both closer and more meaningful than most of those forged earlier in our careers. We attribute this to the style of feedback, the more collaborative approach to growth, and the time we spent simply talking to students about learning and helping them achieve *their* goals in our classes. There were a few minor adjustments that we made to the grade translations, the language of the standards in the rubric, the minimum requirements, and the cumulative exams. We also moved away from numerical levels in the rubric to descriptors like Beginning, Developing, Proficient, and so on. Most of the structure stayed the same because they worked so well: nine practices, content mastery checkpoints, portfolios, conferences, and the types of assessments.

A major, extremely effective change was implementing *benchmarks* (see Figure 4.8). While this is discussed in great detail in Chapter 6, it is worth summarizing here. A common student/parent complaint is "We don't know if we are doing well in this class." Therefore, we defined, *for*

Figure 4.8   Developing

Using benchmarks: Problem solving—Unit 1

	NOT ENOUGH EVIDENCE	BEGINNING	DEVELOPING	PROFICIENT	ADVANCED	EXPERT
Problem solving	I do not attempt to solve the problem described.	I attempt to solve the problem.	I attempt to solve scientific problems and show some relevant supporting work.	I solve scientific problems, showing my supporting work so that someone can follow my thought processes. This means that I show given and variables on a labelled sketch or illustration, diagrams, equations used, numbers plugged in, and can answer.	I select and apply the correct mathematical process to solve physics problems correctly in a familiar context, including all given, variables and answer(s), all with correct units. I can use a calculator properly.	When presented with a complex context, I fully apply the problem-solving methodology to independently solve the problem correctly.

each unit, what is "good progress" for each of the nine standards. In other words, for the first unit of the year, we may expect all students to be trying, and therefore coming in at Beginning, but due to our coaching during that unit, progress to Developing in just two of the nine standards. By the end of the first unit they would be able to say that they were doing well if they had seven Beginning and two Developing scores. To keep the focus on the current level of development, we only reveal the benchmarks for each unit on the rubric, blocking all other criteria from view.

There are a couple of reasons for this change. First, it prevents students from looking ahead and attempting skills they are not yet ready to perform. Second, this prevents our striving learners from getting discouraged by what may seem like an insurmountable task. For the next unit, we would continue at the Developing level for the two standards and work on coaching students to work at the Developing level for a few more. In this way, we would gradually bring students to Proficiency and above, keeping the intrinsic load down, and focusing on gradually climbing the ladder without skipping any of the rungs (see Figure 4.9). The desired achievement levels are given at the beginning of each unit, and support/practice is provided for areas of expected growth. If they meet

Figure 4.9 Proficient

	NOT ENOUGH EVIDENCE	BEGINNING	DEVELOPING	PROFICIENT	ADVANCED	EXPERT
Problem solving	I do not attempt to solve the problem described.	I attempt to solve the problem.	I attempt to solve scientific problems and show some relevant supporting work.	I solve scientific problems, showing my supporting work so that someone can follow my thought processes. This means that I show the given variables on a labeled sketch or illustration, diagrams, equations used, numbers plugged in, and can provide an answer.	I select and apply the correct mathematical process to solve physics problems correctly in a familiar context, including all given, variables and answer(s), all with correct units. I can use a calculator properly.	When presented with a complex context, I fully apply the problem-solving methodology to independently solve the problem correctly.

the benchmark, they can be assured that they are on track for a B or better. If they are below the benchmark, they need support/help during the next unit to catch up and remediate. That gets communicated via our grading platform as well as through individual conferencing. This is a great tool for our planning: if we see that a majority of students are below the benchmark on a particular skill, then we can plan for activities within that unit to work on it. There were plenty of times during this year when we saw that students still were striving to comprehend a particular practice, and so we continued at that level during the next unit, providing additional activities to help students improve. Doing this has enabled students to build stable foundations before attempting to build on them. It also breaks the skill acquisition into manageable portions.

The biggest test of this model began on March 13, 2020. That is the day we were shut down for the remainder of the year due to COVID-19 (coronavirus disease 2019). Although far from an ideal situation, our students continued to engage with the material and learn. The flexibility and adaptability of this model has strengthened our position on the necessity for implementation of more standards-based models.

Creating Language for the Learning Progressions

CHAPTER #5

Now we can get to the practical stuff. Where do you even begin when transitioning to this system?

You've got to begin by identifying your own values as well as those set out by the national standards for your content area. Once you've formulated a set of practices, then you need to develop a progression to distinguish the levels of achievement for each individual practice. What does it look like from the student's point of view? In this chapter we will go in depth on how we've developed the language for our learning progressions and show how this method can be applied to other content areas.

Please note that we will be using examples primarily pulled from our own experience, which is in the science classroom. However, these concepts apply across any and all content areas, and we will address those as well.

Let's work with one of our practices, which we call Creating Explanations and Making Predictions. First, we identified what a perfect response would look like, from a grade-level expert.

> *I can correctly choose and overtly state the relevant physics, in the form of definitions, laws, mathematical models, equations, or relationships. I produce an accurate explanation or prediction that fully ties all of the relevant physics concepts to the correct answer, in an unfamiliar or complex situation. This may require the use of multiple steps and/or multiple Big Ideas, applying previously learned material when necessary.*

Once the Expert level was identified, then we could tease apart the sequence. Someone who was close to the Expert level but not quite there yet may only be able to do those tasks for familiar situations but not for complex or unfamiliar situations. To clarify the levels and remain consistent, we used a focus word.

This allowed us to follow the same progression through each standard as well as to reflect back and assess if we were meeting our intended purpose. Below are these associations:

Beginning => Try

Developing => Explain

Proficient => Explicit

Advanced => Correct

Expert => Complete/Complex

These levels can be envisioned as rungs of a ladder, where the previous step is an essential support in order to make progress up to the top. When fleshing out each standard, we defined what that focus word looked like *in practice* at each developmental level. Let's continue looking at our creating explanations and making predictions standard. We can examine student responses to the following test question:

> A large truck is rear ended by a small compact car. A student says that the change in momentum of the truck is less than the change in momentum of the car. Is this true or false? Explain your reasoning.

You don't have to know much physics to use this scoring scale, honestly. For a student to be assessed as *trying* to answer the question, they must create a response that addresses the question. The Beginning level is worded "I write an explanation or prediction that addresses the reason why I answered the question using information from this unit." Notice that their answer does not need to be correct or include any relevant conceptual knowledge. It is merely attempting to provide an answer. An example of a Beginning-level answer is "*This is true because the truck has a lot more mass and therefore takes more energy to move while the car is a lot lighter and requires less energy to accelerate or stop*" (IK). While this student answers the question by explaining why he thought it was true, he does not use any relevant terminology from the momentum unit. He uses real physics concepts, like mass, energy, and acceleration, but it is not helpful in responding to the question asked.

Explaining requires students to supplement this answer (from the Beginning level) with relevant conceptual terms. Therefore, the Developing level is worded "I use relevant terminology and/or state relevant Big Ideas in my explanation or prediction." Although the answer and the concepts used to generate the answer may still be incorrect, the student is now identifying concepts that are related to the question without elaborating. An example of a Developing-level answer is "*This is true because the law of momentum conservation makes the momentum change the same*" (AS). Contrast this with the previous response, which used irrelevant concepts. In this response the student uses relevant terminology (law of momentum conservation) but does not overtly define what it is or why it makes the momentum change the same.

At the next level, students explicitly define the concept on which their answer is constructed. Therefore, the Proficient level is worded "While making an explanation or prediction, I can correctly choose and overtly state the relevant physics, in the form of definitions, laws, mathematical models, equations, or relationships." The definition of the relevant concept must be overt and correct. However, the application may not be accurate. An example of a Proficient-level answer is *"This is false because the law of conservation of momentum states that the momentum of two objects before a collision is equal to the momentum of the objects after the collision"* (HS). In this response the student not only uses relevant terminology (law of conservation of momentum) but she also overtly defines what it is. However, she does not tie the concept to the answer, so I don't know how she is using the law to determine that it is false. Again, contrast this to the previous answer, and you'll see the difference: she defines the law of conservation of momentum, while the previous student does not.

To progress to the Advanced level, students must provide an explicit definition of the correct concept needed to address the question, as well as accurately answer the question. The Advanced level is worded "I produce an *accurate* explanation or prediction that fully ties all of the relevant physics concepts to the correct answer, in a familiar situation." An example of an Advanced-level answer is *"This is incorrect because the law of conservation of momentum states that the momentum lost by one object is gained by the other object. Therefore, according to the LCM, the total initial p = total final p and the truck will have the same change in momentum as the car"* (DA). In this response the student overtly defines the law correctly. He also ties the concept overtly to the answer, so I clearly see that he is using the law to determine that it is incorrect. It is not complex because the answer depends only on one Big Idea.

For a student to be considered an expert, they must accurately define and apply concepts to a question that involves multiple Big Ideas or steps. Their response must be comprehensive and show a complete understanding of the nuances of the topic. It is worded "I produce an accurate explanation or prediction for a complex situation. This may require the use of multiple steps and/or multiple Big Ideas, applying previously learned material when necessary." This test question could not be answered on the Expert level because it did not require complexity. That was fine for this particular class. However, for a more advanced student or class, a question requiring multiple steps or concepts could be asked. For example, we could change the question to

> A large truck is rear ended by a small compact car. In situation 1 their bumpers tangle, and they move together. In situation 2 the car moves forward separately from the truck. In which case will the car will have a bigger momentum change? Explain your reasoning.

To answer this question, a student would need to use multiple concepts and compare two different scenarios, hence the level of complexity is higher.

We have eight other standards besides the creating explanations and making predictions one, but all are organized in similar fashion: they try => they throw around relevant terminology => they explain the concept overtly => they are correct => they can apply to complex situations. Note that in the descriptors we do not repeat what has already been addressed in a previous level. In other words, if in the Developing level they were to label graph axes with variables and units, then we would not repeat this for any level above that. It is assumed that this criterion must be met to move past Developing; without it the student earns Beginning.

This systematic approach can be used to develop learning progressions for the practices in *any* content area, not just high school science. Here are a few examples from other courses.

Example: History Contextualization

A U.S. history teacher scores contextualization using the rubric in Figure 5.1.

Figure 5.1   History contextualization rubric

Beginning: My response is a phrase or reference related to the prompt.

Developing: My responses provides a specific historical event to support the claim.

Proficient: My response relates the topic of the prompt to a relevant historical event, development, or process.

Advanced: The broader historical event, development, or process is described correctly and in adequate detail. I clearly communicate the time frame of the event relative to the question.

Expert: Fully and accurately describes a broader historical context relevant to the prompt, with multiple supporting events.

Here is the opening paragraph of a three-paragraph essay written by a 10th grader. In this assessment we are looking only at the contextualization of the response. Does this student provide a response that puts the event in the proper historical context, while providing supporting evidence and a correct description of the process of impeachment? It is not until we evaluate the Expert level that a full and accurate accounting of the event as well as a correct and supported explanation of the process are required.

Only two U.S presidents have ever been successfully impeached, meaning this act is very rare. These Presidents were Andrew Johnson and Bill Clinton. In Johnson's case, he went against the Senate's vote and Clinton was charged with perjury and obstruction of justice. But what does that actually mean? Why were they impeached? Contrary to what some may think, impeachment does not mean the President is removed from office; it is simply an investigation that questions the integrity of the actions of the President. Impeachment can be caused by three things: treason, bribery or other high crimes and misdemeanors. Even though impeachment is rare, in 2019 President Donald Trump is the newest candidate for being impeached. After numerous poor political moves for our country, he finally messed up where it hurt him and I believe he should face the consequences and be impeached. President Trump should be impeached because he committed a quid pro quo and was involved with bribery.

This student's claim is the last sentence of the paragraph. Again, let's move through the rubric, starting at the top. She meets the qualifications for Beginning because her response is at least a phrase or reference related to the prompt. She meets the qualifications for Developing because her response provides a specific historical event to support the claim (Johnson and Clinton). She meets the qualifications for Proficient because her response relates the topic of the prompt to a relevant historical event, development, or process. Since the examples are about other impeachments, they are certainly relevant. Does she meet qualifications for Advanced? Because the broader historical process of impeachment is described correctly and in adequate detail, maybe. But she doesn't seem to clearly communicate the time frame of the event relative to the question. This means that she cannot earn Advanced. But I could then explain quite clearly that all she needs to do is add that information and she would be right there! To reiterate, at this level the student is not being evaluated on the accuracy of her interpretation of events but on her explanation of the process of impeachment itself. We are not evaluating the Expert level here, which would require the accuracy of both the process and the interpretation of this specific event.

Example: English Language Arts Thesis/Claim

For an English Language Arts (ELA) class, the teacher may use the rubric given in Figure 5.2 to score the thesis/claim (for any piece of writing).

Figure 5.2   English language arts thesis

Beginning: I respond to the prompt, but I either do not take a position or the position is vague or must be inferred.

Developing: I present a thesis that makes a claim that responds to the prompt.

Proficient: The thesis clearly takes a position rather than just stating that there are pros/cons. My thesis consists of one or more sentences located in one place.

Advanced: The claim/thesis establishes a correct line of reasoning.

Expert: The claim/thesis establishes a defensible interpretation or position.

A student began a six-page paper comparing the novel *To Kill a Mockingbird* with the movie *A Time to Kill* in her ninth-grade English class. Here is the opening paragraph:

> *What could be similar between an American classic novel written in the '60s, "To Kill a Mockingbird", and a late '90s movie, "A Time to Kill"? It is easily assumed that because of the age difference between the book and film there would be mostly differences, but that is not the case. Although they have numerous differences such as different time periods, the similarities between the two are striking. These similarities include the role of a "guardian angel", racist townspeople and the almost identical careers of the two main male characters, Jake and Atticus.*

Let's evaluate her performance on thesis/claim using the rubric. She meets the requirements for Developing because she not only responds to the prompt but also presents a thesis that *makes a claim* that responds to the prompt when she states, *"These similarities include the role of a 'guardian angel,' racist townspeople, and the almost identical careers of the two main male characters, Jake and Atticus."* This statement clearly takes a position and so meets the qualifications for Proficient. Her line of reasoning is correct and therefore is Advanced. Last, we check for Expert by seeing if the thesis/claim establishes a defensible interpretation or position. It can be defended (and will be later on), therefore she earns Expert on this particular skill.

Always start at the lowest levels and work up. If her response was defensible but only stated pros/cons, then she would be at the Developing level. That's why the order of presentation is important, as is uncovering one level at a time.

Example: Math Problem Solving

In a 10th-grade math course, the teacher scores students' problem-solving practice using the rubric given in Figure 5.3.

Figure 5.3   Problem solving

Beginning: I attempt to solve problems.

Developing: I attempt to solve problems using diagrams, equations, and/or variables.

Proficient: I attempt to solve problems using diagrams, equations, and/or variables, showing the solving steps.

Advanced: I correctly solve problems using diagrams, equations, and/or variables, showing the solving steps.

Expert: I correctly solve complex or multistep problems using diagrams, equations, and/or variables, showing the solving steps.

One student submits the solution given in Figure 5.4 to a problem.

Figure 5.4 Solution

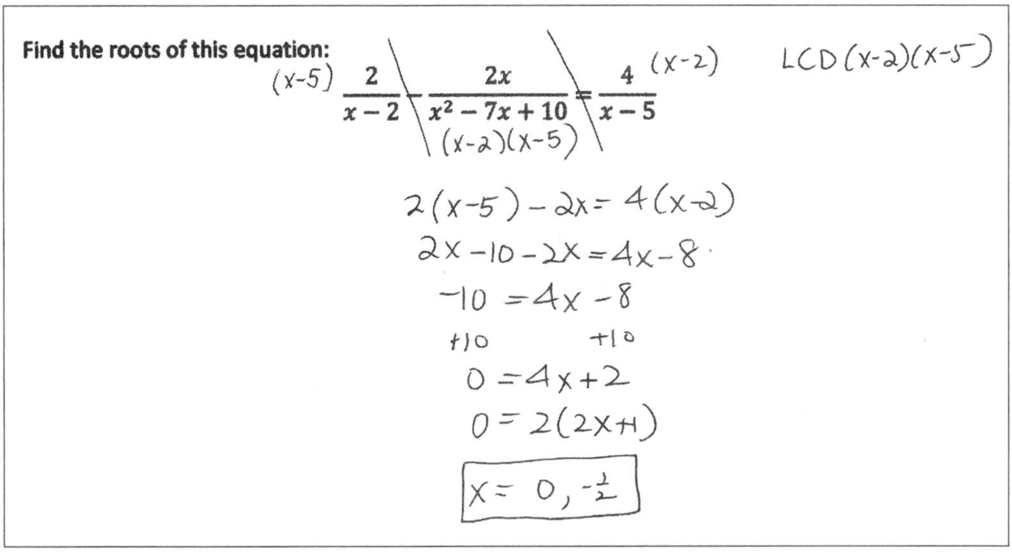

Find the roots of this equation:

$$(x-5)\ \frac{2}{x-2} \Bigg\backslash\ \frac{2x}{x^2-7x+10} \Bigg\backslash\ \frac{4}{x-5}\ (x-2) \qquad LCD\ (x-2)(x-5)$$

$$(x-2)(x-5)$$

$$2(x-5)-2x=4(x-2)$$
$$2x-10-2x=4x-8$$
$$-10=4x-8$$
$$+10 \qquad +10$$
$$0=4x+2$$
$$0=2(2x+1)$$

$$\boxed{x=0,\ -\tfrac{1}{2}}$$

To score this example using the rubric, I would start at Beginning: did she attempt to solve the problem? Yes. Move to Developing: did she use equations, diagrams, and/or variables? Yes, clearly she used equations and variables. To earn Proficient, she should show her solving steps, which she clearly did. Now, is the solution correct? Only one of her answers is correct. Inclusion of the zero as one of the roots is wrong. Therefore, she would earn Proficient on this problem.

Example: Art Elements and Principles

In a Fine Arts class, a teacher tests students on their application of art elements and principles, scoring their progress with the rubric given in Figure 5.5.

Figure 5.5 Art elements

Not enough evidence: I did not attempt.

Beginning: I attempt to demonstrate an art element or principle.

Developing: I can demonstrate an art element or principle from a given example or with teacher guidance.

Proficient: I can demonstrate an art element or principle based on a prompt.

Advanced: I can select a medium/technique that enhances the demonstration of an art element or principle.

Expert: I can accurately explain how the culture, historical period, and/or medium/technique affects the application of the art element or principle.

Students were tasked to create a mixed-media landscape demonstrating knowledge of depth. They were challenged to experiment with and utilize a minimum of four different materials to enhance their overall piece with a focus on texture.

(GH) 10th-Grade Student

This student satisfied the Beginning level by attempting to demonstrate depth and texture (see Figure 5.6). Since this is the student's original work, not based on an example and without teacher input and guidance, it satisfied both the Developing and the Proficient level. The materials chosen to demonstrate texture do not enhance the overall texture of this piece. Therefore, the rating in this standard is Proficient.

Figure 5.6   Art work, 10th grader

(GC) 11th-Grade Student

This student demonstrated the principles of depth and texture in an original piece, without assistance or guidance from the teacher, satisfying the Beginning, Developing, and Proficient levels (see Figure 5.7). In contrast to the previous work, the size, shape, and placement of the materials within this composition enhance the depth of the piece. The texture of the materials chosen helps create a natural atmosphere, bringing this piece to the Advanced level. Through follow-up responses, it was revealed that the student did not correlate the piece with any cultural or historical contexts, which prevents this work from being rated at the Expert level.

Figure 5.7   Art work, 11th grader

Painting by Gabby Cabrera

In each of these examples we have shown how a response fulfills a single standard. However, many times one artifact will be assessed on several standards. For example, only the opening paragraph of the history essay was presented to show how one would use the contextualization standard. However, typically, an open-ended response to a prompt may also be assessed on a thesis, evidence, or presentation/style standard. Similarly, an entire lab report may also be assessed on several aspects, such as experimental design, data analysis, and creating a scientific argument. There are plentiful examples in the resources. In Resources A you will find examples of student work and how these rubrics (and more) were used to score the work. In Resources B you will see how one student's work on a particular standard developed over the course of the year. In Resources C you will find rubrics for several courses, each more fully fleshed out with several practices. The key here is to use words that clearly communicate what evidence of expertise you are looking for at each level, without creating a checklist or prescription.

Assessments

CHAPTER #6

Introduction

All instructors assess their students, both formally and informally. We intend to be objective, measuring against seemingly unbiased standards. But there is *no context that is not subjective* in some aspect. You might be thinking, "That's not true! 1 + 1 = 2, and that's either right or wrong. That's not a teacher's opinion!" So let's suppose that the student writes "1 + 1 = 3." If the teacher is interested in measuring student ability to write an equation or solve a word problem, then the focus may not be on the mathematics at all. Did they write an equation? Yes. Is the sum correct? No. What is the teacher assessing: that the student knows the format for an equation, how to pull information out of a word problem, or how to do correct sums? Each teacher subjectively chooses to award points for different products.

Setting the Stage: Our Past Practice

Most of us do not overtly spell out the details, *even to ourselves*, of what we are actually assessing. As physics teachers we emphasized problem solving throughout our course. We taught students how to set up problems, assigning point values to each piece. It was important to us that students learn how to set up a problem because while some problems are easy and don't usually require much work to find a correct answer, more difficult problems absolutely do. Students need to learn a problem-solving strategy on the simple tasks in order to apply it to more complex ones. So we would assign 2 points for the labeled diagram, 1 point for choosing the correct equation, another point for plugging in the correct values into that equation, and a single point for the answer as long as it had correct units (see Figure 6.1). Obviously, more complex problems were worth more points.

Note that the point values were completely arbitrary and *up to the teacher*. Making a calculation error or forgetting units on the answer resulted in 80% of points earned if the other steps were completed correctly; having only the correct answer with units but no supporting work earned 20%. These point values, we argued, showed students what we valued and trained them to complete the steps we think are really important.

And it worked. We could move most students from showing no work to presenting organized work. But here's the problem we encountered:

Figure 6.1 Sample point valuation

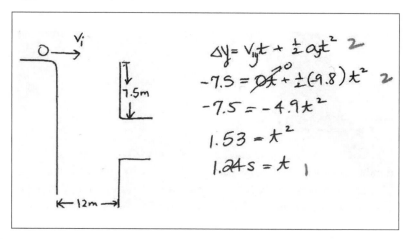

if any of the steps were wrong, they earned no points for that step. It was all about being right. This is very discouraging for most students but especially for our striving students. In addition, while most students were very compliant, obeying our rules because we said so, they didn't understand *why* it was important. In the end if they were wrong, they didn't get good scores. What about the students who are close but make minor mistakes? Those who understand the *process* of problem solving but have trouble executing the mathematics? Regardless of those inherent issues, the resulting conversation was "What grade did I get?" and judgment reigned based on that grade.

Why Did It Need to Change?

Here are six major concerns that have been raised about the traditional system of grading:

1. *An obsession with grades:* Students (and parents) are fixated on grades. In elementary school it's about getting ready for middle school; in middle school everyone is worried about getting ready for high school; in high school it's about college entry; and in college it's about the job/career/grad school. While none of these concerns are invalid, at what point is school about mastering skills? Students learn early on that people will simply judge them based on their grades. According to Jo Boaler and Carol Dweck (2016) in *Mathematical Mindsets*, grading reduces the achievement of students, even when accompanied by feedback, and produces an identity associated with the score. What is meant by identity? It is not just "I am a math person" or "I am a bad writer" but also a value judgment. Girls especially will equate their school performance with being a good or a bad person. When students are merely working for a grade, school can be entirely uninteresting, stressful, and a source

of dissatisfaction. Curiosity, creativity, and risk taking are muffled if not extinguished, especially for striving students. How many times have we heard from students that they are "bad test takers"? Experts acknowledge that lower levels of achievement are the result of striving for a grade; grades are not a good source of motivation (Boaler & Dweck, 2016).

Obsession with grades is part of the culture of our schools, of our media, and of our country. You hear it constantly within your classes as well as in the national dialogue about performance.

2. *Stress:* The traditional approach leads to unnecessary student stress. Let us be clear. We are not opposed to stress. It is important for students to experience and learn how to manage stress, but if we can eliminate situations that are *unnecessarily* stressful, it will allow students to experience productive stress, take academic risks, and focus on learning. The documentaries *Race to Nowhere* (Abeles & Congdon, 2010) and *Beyond Measure* (Abeles, 2014) both fully flesh out the modern situation and its ramifications.

3. *Inequity:* Assessments were a judgment on the ability and knowledge of a student, based on the information we presented. Regardless of intention, grades were labels we placed on them. We used these labels in our conversations and as a means for recommendations to future courses. This has been more fully addressed in Chapter 2.

4. *Inaccurate feedback regarding skills and expertise:* Without fail we would identify students who didn't match their label. For example, a student who participated fully and interacted with the material might earn a C even though they markedly improved over the year, and be penalized because of the rate of knowledge acquisition. There were students with lower grades who we knew had acquired more skills and knowledge than other students who had higher grades but never improved from the beginning of the year. The final grade just wasn't always an accurate evaluation of student improvement and final levels of achievement.

5. *Time spent grading:* Grading using a points basis takes an inordinate amount of a teacher's time and energy, which can be better used to design the learning experiences and artifacts. Grading can suck the joy out of teaching. It can ruin evenings and weekends. It can heighten our stress level. It can prevent us from giving timely feedback to students; the more detail we want to provide, the longer it takes to grade.

6. *Doesn't reflect the reality of mastering anything:* You can think about child development: how long a child spends crawling versus walking varies widely from one child to another. However, there is no penalty for crawling for six months instead of one month! If a child skips crawling altogether, that doesn't necessarily foreshadow their future athletic success. Both children learn to walk before the end of the year but do it at their own pace. Why should learning in a school setting be any different?

7. *The lasting impact of authentic feedback:* In a traditional approach any single assessment, no matter what time of the year, can have lasting effects on the overall grade at the end of the year. This often made us cautious or even scared to give students accurate feedback. Have you ever regraded tests, manipulating the points so that students would do "better"? Therefore, the grade (A, B, C, D, or F) did not provide true feedback in terms of the specific strengths and weaknesses of the student or any information about how the assessment was conducted.

These seven issues are all addressed in the design and implementation of our *going gradeless* approach.

Addressing the Concerns Regarding the New Structure

When we implement a standards-based grading system, there is a shift in the purpose of assessment. Let's return to the problem-solving techniques described earlier. How did we reimagine/transform that lesson into this feedback-oriented approach? To move students into understanding *the process* while removing the stress of being right, we broke the problem-solving skill down into developmental chunks. First, one must simply try. Often, striving students won't even try because they don't get any credit in the traditional model. So this is where we hook most striving students—imagine their pleasure in getting credit for just making an attempt! Then they might start writing down some relevant information, maybe choosing an equation and plugging some numbers pulled from the word problem. They may get nervous or insecure about their mathematical abilities and may not actually generate an answer. That's fine, because they are showing us that they know *what is relevant*, even if they aren't completely sure how to *use* that information. That's our Developing level. At the next level students draw a labeled diagram, write out a relevant equation, and plug numbers in. There may be mistakes littered throughout these steps, both by omission and by conceptual error, but they clearly know the *process* and can show us that they know what it is. The next level is to correct those mistakes and get the problem right. At the Expert level students have the mastery to apply this strategy to complex problems.

There is a learning model called Assessment for Learning (A4L; Boaler, 2020), which is used internationally. This system defines a good assessment as one that has three main characteristics:

1. It clearly communicates to students what they have learned.

2. It helps students become aware of where they are in their learning journey and where they need to reach.

3. It gives students information on ways to close the gap.

This is exactly what we are trying to do with our learning progressions: communicate where the students currently stand, where they want to get to next, and how to move from one level to another. We do this with a finite number of skills that thread through all our units in all of our courses.

In a traditional classroom, assessment can be used as a ranking system, a gotcha, a determination of "rightness." In a standards-based classroom, assessment is merely feedback on a discrete number of skills and should, if done well, provide information on where the student is on the path to mastery. In this light, many opportunities for feedback are provided. In our classroom this has gone through many iterations—from allowing retakes, to minimum requirements, to peer reviewing. Currently, we have settled on a multifaceted approach that allows students to work on all nine standards many times over the course of the year. Each attempt replaces the previous attempt. There is no penalty for doing poorly along the path to mastery.

Our criteria for assessment design includes opportunities to show that documentation of thought processes is more valuable than providing a right answer. Explanations and proof of work are mandatory and highly valued. Multiple approaches may work and are acceptable. Responses require complex and/or novel applications and thought, as opposed to simply memorizing an answer. Most especially, we design questions that have not only a "low floor" so that everyone can participate and contribute but also a "high ceiling" to provide challenge and interest for those ready to engage at that level. When appropriate, social construction of knowledge is a part of the learning process, using both group and individual accountability.

When we give a percentage or overall grade, the particulars of what students are doing well and what they are doing poorly are lost. Unfortunately, students (and parents) look at the assignment grade and think only about its effect on their average, not what it indicates about their mastery of skills or content. "Work harder" is not a solution; doing more of the same thing will not cause any change. Saying that a student is proficient in problem solving has meaning. It means that they can work on advanced skills next. Saying that she is at the Beginning level on graph interpretation means that there are some gaps in her skills that may need extra help from the coach (aka teacher).

This new format has had a positive effect on students, parents, and teachers. That isn't to say that there weren't growing pains and pushback! However, let's take a hard look at some significant areas of positive impact, namely curriculum design, student mindset, grading, and communication, among others.

On Curriculum and Planning

Prior to this switch, we presented our traditional curriculum, reworking lessons and activities in an attempt to make them more effective. The goal of the course was to cover as much of the curriculum as time would allow, while offering an engaging and educational experience based on core skills. By curriculum we mean topics, which in our courses are heavily content oriented. However, as our mindset changed, so did our assessments. As discussed previously, we now view assessments as feedback and a guide to student progress. This shift occurred naturally once we had clearly defined outcomes for the course. With these clearly defined outcomes, assessments have become more focused and relevant and easier to score. We evaluated every lesson, lab, quiz, test, and project to ensure that they were aligned with our expected outcomes. Any assignment that did not clearly or effectively support these goals was modified or discarded. This was difficult to do because we had some fun, engaging, and successful lessons that were no longer relevant to our new goals and therefore simply had to be discarded. Everything that we present to students now has a purpose that is easily communicated. As mentioned in Chapter 4, the sequence of the course was modified as a result of creating a clear progression of skills. We identified skills and knowledge that needed to be acquired in order to be successful on future outcomes. Then we looked through our library of activities and selected those that build those foundational skills. Through our evaluation of lessons and labs, we determined which assignments highlighted particular skills more effectively than others. Our current arrangement provides a scaffold that is logical in terms of both skill and process. Every assignment has a corresponding rubric that identifies the skills embedded in the lessons. We were able to simplify the types of assessments to three that would address all nine skills: checkpoints (aka quizzes and tests), labs, and projects. More details about those are given later in this chapter.

On Sustained Effort

There is inherent value in simply building skills over time; if you do poorly in a particular context, you are not bad at it; you just haven't mastered it yet. We have no hesitation using coaches for sports and music and gradually building skills over the course of years. For many students (as well as their parents), if a particular skill isn't easy, then the child is simply not talented and should do something different instead. However, it is working hard and for sustained periods of time that is necessary to truly master something. We think that our approach supports this more natural and realistic thinking about success and achievement, while accommodating individual differences and needs. All of this is valuable, creating successful students who can overcome obstacles, adapt to the changing world around them, and be ready for careers that don't even exist yet.

A Note Regarding Integrity

A major concern for some teachers, understandably, is the prospect of cheating. We have been very interested to note that implementing this system has drastically reduced copying and plagiarism on all assignments. As the only outcome for each assessment is feedback, there is no incentive to cheat. There is no long-term benefit to a student's grade, since each score is replaced by the next one. Should we notice an incident of cheating, it is simply an opportunity for discussion and growth. Perhaps the penalty is that the assignment will not count toward that student's minimum requirements, which may put pressure on them to complete additional tasks that they otherwise might have skipped. Because the assessment scores are simply progress reports, individual scores have no direct impact on the student's overall grade until the very last one.

Scalable and Progressive

When we design assessments, we first begin with the standards (as opposed to the topics) that we want to assess. We have designed a pretty systematic approach for each unit that allows us to provide a wide range of assessment opportunities, cycling through 6–10 units, depending on the course level. Not every assessment allows students to achieve the maximum level—for example, in unit 1, students can only earn a maximum level of Developing on standard 4, but by unit 3, they can earn Advanced if they are ready to perform at this level. This has to do with the nature of the questions as well as the sequence of coaching that has to occur. The same happens throughout a unit. For example, we gave a checkpoint in January in which students could not earn more than a Developing on a graphical analysis question; but if they earned the maximum that they could earn, that was just fine. As the designer of the assessment you just need to be clear about what is "good" performance on that particular assessment and then clearly communicate that to students so they learn that the scores reflect particular skills listed on the rubric and are not based on good versus bad, smart versus stupid, or A versus F.

On Grading (Time, Stress, and Feedback)

We can tell you with joy that we spend *a lot less time* grading individual assignments. That doesn't mean that the students aren't getting valuable feedback constantly; they are. First of all, there is simply less to grade, since we have not only pruned the course down to what is essential for achieving our goals but also integrated a lot of guided self-assessment and peer reviewing into the course. Second, the standards are so well honed that it is fairly easy to see a student's level of performance at a glance. We can go through a class set of labs in about a third of the time it used to take, because it's a more holistic and focused approach. It becomes very easy, for example, to find the boundary between a Developing and a Proficient response. Third, we have a lot less stress about giving accurate and honest feedback. Because our scoring does not have any long-term effect on an end-of-the-year grade, we don't have to feel badly about reporting to a student that they haven't met the requirements. We can be honest about where they are and support them in their growth. As a bonus we get to define "late work" as work handed in after we have completed scoring the assignment. We do not score late work; we are way too busy scoring the next thing or designing lessons to do that. However, there is no penalty as there are so many opportunities for future assignments with the same standards. But we are sure to emphasize that the student has missed out on feedback from his or her instructional coach. Some of them will ask to sit with us one-on-one to go over it and get feedback (and we like doing that!), but most won't.

You might also think that giving good feedback requires a lot more time. We have not found it to be so. Mostly, the descriptors in the rubric make it pretty clear what is required, so we can simply point to an omission keeping the student from the next level. But we mainly want to talk to students about their performance. Usually, we simply write an invitation to conference with us in order to go over the work so we can teach them individually what they personally need to do to improve.

When we initially gave assessments, there was a lot of repetition and overlap because our learning outcomes were unclear. The assessments actually helped us refine the standards as we clarified what we were looking for and how to ask questions that could elicit those types of responses.

We can still feel initially disappointed by the results on an assessment because so few students get problems "right." Of course, we want students to learn well and quickly. But the reality is that learning is nonlinear. By tracking their progress through the units to have a wider view, we are pleasantly surprised to see that most students actually make systematic progress across the rubric (see Figures 6.2 and 6.3).

Figure 6.2   Tracking college preparatory average

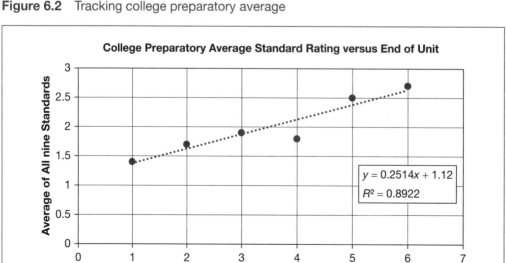

Figure 6.3 Tracking advanced placement

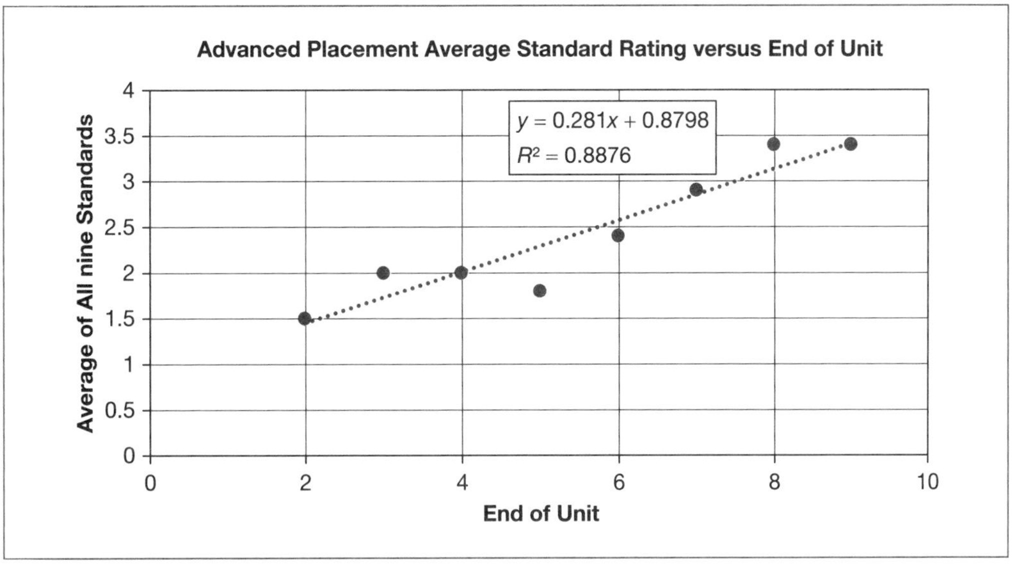
Advanced Placement Average Standard Rating versus End of Unit
y = 0.281x + 0.8798
R2 = 0.8876
Average of All nine Standards
End of Unit
0
0.5
1
1.5
2
2.5
3
3.5
4
0
2
4
6
8
10

Note: For the purposes of data analysis we associated the levels of performance with a numerical value. For example, Expert = 5, Advanced = 4, and so on.

Over the course of the school year, students in this course moved from Beginning to Developing and plateaued there for a while as they assimilated all of the skills needed for proficiency. By unit 5, more than half the students were at the Proficient level and moving on to Advanced.

Let's look at one student throughout the entire year of an AP Physics 1 course. Don't worry about the complexity of the problems, but just look at the student's progress on our problem-solving standard (see Figure 6.4).

Figure 6.4 Student response 1

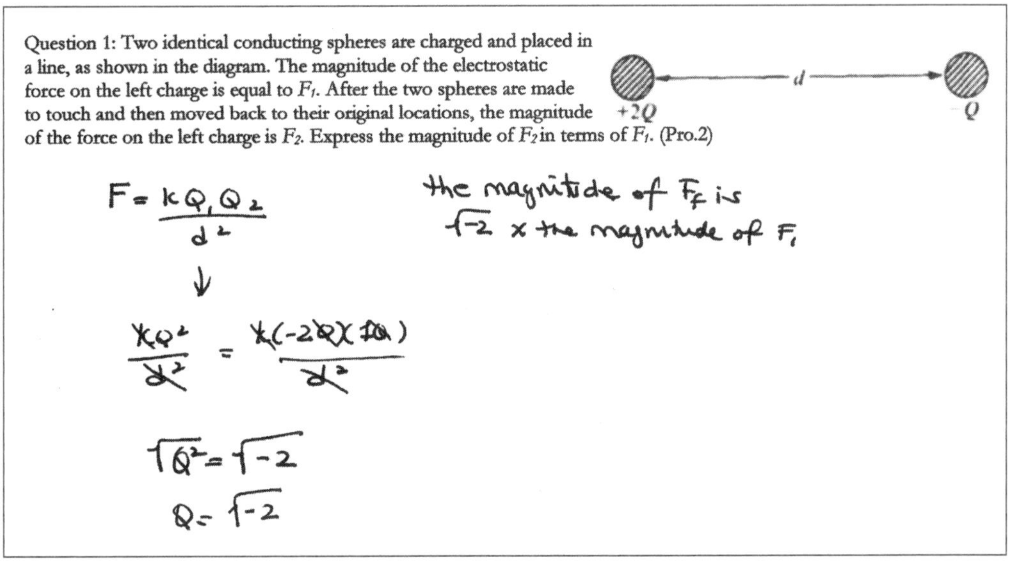
Question 1: Two identical conducting spheres are charged and placed in a line, as shown in the diagram. The magnitude of the electrostatic force on the left charge is equal to F1. After the two spheres are made to touch and then moved back to their original locations, the magnitude of the force on the left charge is F2. Express the magnitude of F2 in terms of F1. (Pro.2)
+2Q
d
Q
the magnitude of F2 is
√-2 x the magnitude of F1

At the start of the year this student earned a Developing level because she didn't answer the question, although she had relevant equations and variables shown.

In unit 3, notice how her response is more organized. She earned Proficient because she had a labeled diagram and showed all her work, even though there were several errors (see Figure 6.5).

Figure 6.5   Student response 2

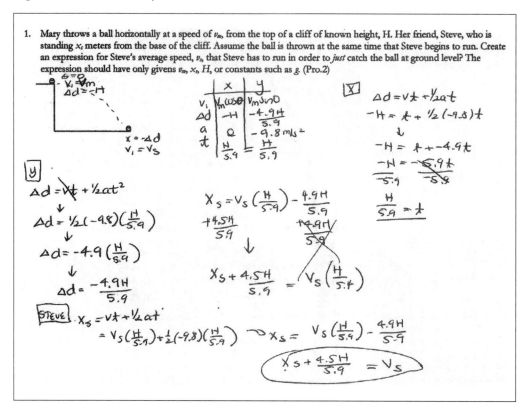

1. Mary throws a ball horizontally at a speed of v_m, from the top of a cliff of known height, H. Her friend, Steve, who is standing x_i meters from the base of the cliff. Assume the ball is thrown at the same time that Steve begins to run. Create an expression for Steve's average speed, v_s, that Steve has to run in order to *just* catch the ball at ground level? The expression should have only givens v_m, x_i, H, or constants such as g. (Pro.2)

Many high-performing students often stall at the Proficient level for a while as it takes time to master the problem-solving approach. They are usually so consumed about getting a right answer to these very challenging problems that they panic and flail about instead of using a systematic approach. It takes some time before they are confident enough in the process to start getting the problems correct. Here she is in unit 5 still earning Proficient. Notice that she labeled very little on the diagram; although her work looks impressive, completion of this step is required, regardless of the accuracy of the remainder of the problem (see Figure 6.6). This requirement builds support for the complex problems that these students will encounter on the AP exam.

Figure 6.6   Student response 3

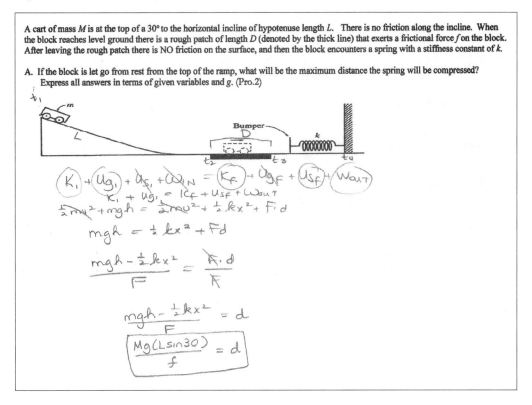

A cart of mass M is at the top of a 30° to the horizontal incline of hypotenuse length L.   There is no friction along the incline. When the block reaches level ground there is a rough patch of length D (denoted by the thick line) that exerts a frictional force f on the block. After leaving the rough patch there is NO friction on the surface, and then the block encounters a spring with a stiffness constant of k.

A. If the block is let go from rest from the top of the ramp, what will be the maximum distance the spring will be compressed? Express all answers in terms of given variables and g. (Pro.2)

By the end of the year she was producing much more complete work, with labeled diagrams and clear communication (see Figure 6.7). This was a very challenging and complex problem, with an error. However, due to the clear communication in problem solving, it was easy to determine where the error was made, which means she earned Advanced.

Seeing this type of real, measurable progress is infinitely rewarding, and more important, it is very stable. Once a skill is mastered, it can be applied to a wide variety of situations, and that engenders a confidence that cannot be achieved through merely earning a good grade.

On Conversations With Students and Parents

During each assignment and on submission of the associated artifact, students receive verbal and written feedback. This feedback pertains to the level of skill they currently exhibit, their rate of growth, and the next steps necessary for progression through the standards. We emphasize incremental improvement over time. The immediate concern is how to make the next submission an improvement over the current submission. We try to eliminate the concept of *right* or *wrong*, replacing it with

Figure 6.7   Student response 4

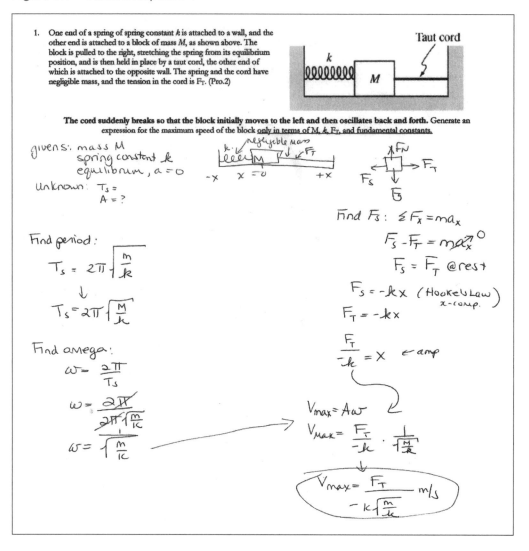

reasonable or *unreasonable*. The goal is to make students aware of *why* they are making the choices they are making. They can then self-assess by asking, "Are my choices supporting my desired outcome?" This is in agreement with the growth mindset movement, which postulates that all students *can* learn high-level content but each student has his or her own needs and pace. If students know that they have time to practice, to make mistakes, and to improve without penalty, they will de-emphasize grades and start focusing on the process. In our classrooms we have noticed that students try harder and take just as much time and effort to complete a test (or project or lab) that has absolutely no direct impact on their final grade. They are willing to complete most assignments without stressing about perfection. We get much less pushback about the open-ended nature of our assessments and high-level questioning because students know that they only need to show progress, not be perfect.

Our Types of Assessments

We are going to go into some detail about the three types of assessments that we use in our classroom. Obviously, depending on your course, you will have your own categories. But we thought that it would be useful to take you through the decision-making and reasoning for each one, as well as the benefits we've experienced.

Checkpoints and Tests

Students take weekly checkpoints, which are essentially quizzes worth 0 points. We moved away from the term *quiz* because quizzes have always been associated with grades. We did not want students to get the impression that these were more important than any other practice that they do. When we were administering assessments for points, we had to make sure that we had enough questions, worth enough points to make sure that the quiz was weighted properly in our overall grading scheme. We no longer have to concern ourselves with points and the number of questions. We can now focus on developing fewer, more effective questions that incorporate the skills we are assessing. This shortens the length of the checkpoint to less than half a period. If a student doesn't finish within this time, that is a lesson—that they haven't mastered the material well enough to work quickly. At the conclusion of the checkpoint, each question is reviewed on the board as a class. Students switch the writing instrument they had used to take the checkpoint and make corrections and take copious notes based on the teacher-led, in-class review of the questions. The opportunity to provide *immediate feedback* is a core requirement for student engagement. It is important that it is fresh enough in their minds so that they recall their original thoughts and can note down corrections or enhancements to their responses. We take them through the rubric, asking guiding questions to help them identify where they land on the learning progressions for each standard. They score *themselves* based on the rubric provided for that specific checkpoint. In doing so they learn how to use the rubric and what it says, as well as the distinguishing characteristics between levels.

Tests are nearly identical in structure to checkpoints, although approached in a slightly different manner. Students can have a full period if they wish, therefore the responses cannot be reviewed together immediately. However, the same rubric is provided at the top of the page and can be used for guidance during the test. The scoring is done by the teacher as opposed to the student. There are two reasons for the external scoring: one is to provide a model of constructive criticism and useful feedback for the student; the second is to provide the teacher with a compass reading of how the class (or individual student) is performing so we can adjust our teaching. Regardless, the main emphasis of any assessment is incremental growth and improvement. Identification of weaknesses is only useful to address them in the subsequent unit. (We do not retest.)

Projects

Because the NGSS has a stated emphasis on engineering design, and because physics really lends itself to model construction, one of our standards is about the engineering design process. Each unit has an open-ended project with parameters and rules; their job is not just to meet the basic requirements but to also optimize their results. Since it is introduced on the first day of the unit, students will typically have six weeks until the due date. Within the first few days they make their first prototype. Their next prototype ideally addresses a clearly identified shortcoming of the first with a scientific approach (only changing one variable at a time). This process should continue throughout the unit as they learn more physics content. They do not compete with each other; they compete with their own previous model. Throughout the project they must keep a log of their activity, maintain a documentation of each iteration, and specify the reasons why they made the alterations to their product. This allows us to assess their planning, peer interactions, and application of concepts. Components and concepts of earlier projects are used as the base for future projects, culminating in a final project that assesses the skills developed throughout the year.

Laboratory Experiments

Being a science class, it will come as no surprise that students spend a lot of time designing labs, collecting and analyzing data, and writing conclusions. We do well over 15 per year, which gives students plenty of practice. These used to be the bane of our grading, taking hours of the weekend to read these artifacts. Using the outcomes has really given students a lot of direction. This is the area in which I see the most progress with students. Labs are still a lot of work, but most of them really understand why they are doing what they are doing and produce very impressive documents. In addition to the guidance from the outcomes, one of the major reasons for the increase in the quality of these submissions is the use of working memory in our assessment design. Previously, we had presented all the components of a lab report, assessed them, and provided feedback on how to improve each of them. Our new assessment model allows us to assess individual parts of the lab in a meaningful way. We start with "arguing scientific claims" (our conclusion) because of the lower intrinsic load. Students are generally familiar with this concept from their ELA classes, which makes it easier for us to expand their level of proficiency in a science context. We will continue to assess this practice until students are maintaining the Proficient level. Only at that point will we introduce the next lab skill, assessing that until proficiency is met. By introducing each practice individually, we don't exceed the student's working memory.

Aligning Progress With a Traditional Model

The big question is "How do we fit this model into a traditional framework?" While our particular administration is highly supportive of our goals, at the end of the semester we too have to post grades A to F. In this chapter we will demonstrate how our three-pronged approach—minimum requirements, progress on all nine of our process standards, and individual conferencing, all detailed in Chapter 4—is used to address this quandary. In the process we will dig deeply into common questions about tracking, grade translations, and scaling for course leveling.

Let's set the stage by first summarizing a typical, more traditional model of the classroom. In most classrooms students receive individual grades on each assignment and some type of averaging happens. Generally, a percentage is reported, ranging from 0% to 100%, associated with A–F (with pluses or minuses, depending on the district). Anything below 60% is considered an F, or failure, and the class must be retaken.

In contrast, with our gradeless system every assessment is a snapshot of the skills demonstrated when that assessment was done. What do we use instead of an average of all graded assignments at the end of the year? We use a final unit in which the theme is an engaging project. During these last three to four weeks of school, students have several opportunities to produce work that measurably assesses each of our nine skills. There is no new content delivered, but an application of several bodies of knowledge taught during the previous nine months of school. Therefore, the very last assessment of each standard is a true demonstration of accumulated skills *at that point in time.*

Grade Translations

Schools are like all institutions: by definition, they are slow to change. Until the reporting (and the mindset) adapts to our needs, we have to be prepared to work within its constraints. One of the most common questions that we field in workshops is how to use a standards-based model even when the rest of the school is not using one. How does one translate these descriptive outcomes to a letter grade? We struggled with this at first but came up with a great solution.

In our Physics classes, students are assessed on our nine process standards (see Resources C). These are published for students and parents to view in our gradebook (Genesis) and learning management system (Canvas), or LMS, on day 1 of the school year. These competencies are continually assessed from September through June, with detailed feedback provided at every assessment. Our expectation is that students will exhibit *incremental improvement* over the course of the year. As described in Chapter 4, we set benchmarks regarding the expected performance for each unit, but all that students have to do is continually and gradually develop skills over time. The grade reported *at any point in the year* should be viewed only as a *progress report* of where the student is *at that moment*. Due to this expectation, the final scores will be based solely on the most current submissions, those assessed during the last weeks of school.

How achievement in the nine competencies is translated to a course grade is illustrated in the charts in Figures 7.1 and 7.2. The first chart is the progress reporting in January (end of the first semester; Figure 7.1), and the second one is the final grade at the end of the school year (Figure 7.2).

How do we use this scale? For example, let's say a Physics student has earned five standards at the Developing level and the other four at the Proficient level. Using the chart in Figure 7.2, first find the rows that show "With no standard lower than Developing" (see Figure 7.3).

Then use the left-hand column to find the highest level of achievement. If this student has four at the Proficient level, he or she has three but hasn't earned six, so this means that he or she earns a B– at the end of the year. How can teachers help students use this as a tool for

Figure 7.1 Midyear translation

At the end of the semester (January), for a student taking Physics

PROCESS STANDARD SCORE REQUIREMENTS TOTAL OF . . .	MINIMUM REQUIREMENTS	WILL EARN A PROGRESS REPORT OF . . .
Any 3 standards at Advanced level	With no standard lower than Proficient	A+
All standards at Proficient level	With no standard lower than Proficient	A
Any 8 standards at Proficient level	With no standard lower than Developing	A–
Any 5 standards at Proficient level	With no standard lower than Developing	B+
Any 2 standards at Proficient level	With no standard lower than Developing	B
All standards at Developing level	With no standard lower than Developing	B–
Any 8 standards at Developing level	With no standard lower than Beginning	C+
Any 5 standards at Developing level	With no standard lower than Beginning	C
Any 2 standards at Developing level	With no standard lower than Beginning	C–
Met all minimum course requirements	With no standard lower than Beginning	D
Not enough evidence to evaluate 1 or more standards		F

Figure 7.2 End-of-course translation

At the end of the school year (June), for a student taking Physics:

OUT OF 10 PROCESS STANDARDS, EARN . . .	MINIMUM REQUIREMENTS	WILL EARN AN END-OF-YEAR COURSE GRADE OF . . .
Any 9 standards at Advanced level	With no standard lower than Proficient	A+
Any 6 standards at Advanced level	With no standard lower than Proficient	A
Any 3 standards at Advanced level	With no standard lower than Proficient	A−
Any 9 standards at Proficient level	With no standard lower than Developing	B+
Any 6 standards at Proficient level	With no standard lower than Developing	B
Any 3 standards at Proficient level	With no standard lower than Developing	B−
Any 9 standards at Developing level	With no standard lower than Beginning	C+
Any 6 standards at Developing level	With no standard lower than Beginning	C
Any 3 standards at Developing level	With no standard lower than Beginning	C−
Met all minimum course requirements	With no standard lower than Beginning	D
Not enough evidence to evaluate 1 or more standards		F

Figure 7.3 Using the translation

OUT OF 10 PROCESS STANDARDS, EARN . . .	MINIMUM REQUIREMENTS	WILL EARN AN END-OF-YEAR COURSE GRADE OF . . .
Any 9 standards at Advanced level	With no standard lower than Proficient	A+
Any 6 standards at Advanced level	With no standard lower than Proficient	A
Any 3 standards at Advanced level	With no standard lower than Proficient	A−
Any 9 standards at Proficient level	With no standard lower than Developing	B+
Any 6 standards at Proficient level	With no standard lower than Developing	B
Any 3 standards at Proficient level	With no standard lower than Developing	B−
Any 9 standards at Developing level	With no standard lower than Beginning	C+
Any 6 standards at Developing level	With no standard lower than Beginning	C
Any 3 standards at Developing level	With no standard lower than Beginning	C−
Met all minimum course requirements	With no standard lower than Beginning	D
Not enough evidence to evaluate 1 or more standards		F

learning? We would coach that student, noting that with two additional standards at the Proficient level, B– changes to a B. The student needs to move two skills from Developing to Proficient. Which ones does he or she want to work on? And then we would look at individual work to pinpoint specific changes that could be made. Note that this does not require getting two more questions correct; it means identifying two skills that are weak and making them stronger in demonstrable and clearly implementable ways.

There are a few features worth highlighting here. First of all, notice that the semester benchmarks are "easier" than the end-of-year ones. Hopefully that seems logical to you. Students have only had half of the school year to assimilate and perform the skills; after another five months they should be able to move to a higher level of achievement. Progress is often swift earlier in the course as the ladder rungs are closer together. Higher in the learning progression there are a lot of pieces to put together, so that moving from Proficient to Advanced is a bigger step, taking more time to assimilate.

Let's look at a specific example. To earn a B+ for the midyear grade, a student must earn at least five standards at the Proficient level, with the remaining standards at a minimum of Developing level (see Figure 7.4).

Figure 7.4   B+ requirements midyear

Any 5 standards at Proficient level	With no standard lower than Developing	B+

Getting those same scores in June (aka no improvement) would earn a B– (see Figure 7.5); the next level up, a B, requires six Proficient, not five.

Figure 7.5   B– requirements end of course

Any 3 standards at Proficient level	With no standard lower than Developing	B–

The student has not grown over the five months of school, therefore the score translates to a lower grade. Our goal is growth!

Therefore, to maintain a B+, that student is required to move four more standards up to the Proficient level (see Figure 7.6).

Figure 7.6   B+ requirements end of course

Any 9 standards at Proficient level	With no standard lower than Developing	B+

This is a manageable task for a student working conscientiously and systematically from February through June.

By now you will have noticed that the course grades are steps in a ladder, as opposed to a continuous scale. Moving from a B to a B+ requires earning three more Proficient-level standards, not just one. Therefore, any students earning six, seven, or eight standards at the Proficient level with nothing lower than Developing will earn a B. This is consistent with how the traditional model has a range of scores between 83 and 86 all translated into a B.

Another important aspect to note is that students need to complete the minimum requirements in order to pass (get a D in the traditional model). As discussed in Chapter 4, these are the interactions and assessments that we consider to be the absolute minimum work that we would need to see in order to say that the student took our Physics class and passed. For us, this included a foundational knowledge of all the relevant vocabulary, completion of all seven projects and unit tests, submission of at least 14 of 20 formal lab reports, and meeting for at least two out of the three one-on-one conferences. Students don't have to do these things *well*, but they must be completed. Our justification is that without students doing these things, we would not have enough information to effectively evaluate their learning. And once we set these minimum requirements as the foundation of the course, we were able to figure out how to move them through the learning progressions.

For example, in September, when we are teaching students how to write a lab report, we have them do a sequence of five labs, with explicit guidance (no independence). They score their own product using the rubric, but the expectation is that they will achieve Beginning level on experimental design, Beginning level on data analysis, and Developing level on arguing a scientific claim. If they achieve those levels during unit 1, they are on the right track. However, if they *stay* at that level at the end of unit 2, it may be an indication that we need to approach their learning from a different angle. As time moves on, we will coach them to higher skill levels. Since it is where they end up in June that will determine their final grade in the course, there is no pressure on teachers or on students to master the skill faster than they are able to.

It should be mentioned here that there are two positive side benefits to this system: student goal setting and easy adjustments by the teacher. We cannot ignore the fact that students and parents are used to letter grades. Our grade translations still allow students to set these grade-oriented goals but couch them as specific learning targets. Since the grade is based on mastery of skills, they have to examine the rubric to see what they have to produce in order to hit that target, and choose what personal challenges they need to address. It's not just a numbers game anymore! They must master each standard to the benchmark that we have set. Another benefit of this type of grading is that the teacher can make adjustments when confronted with unforeseen circumstances, such as when we had to suddenly shift to full remote in March 2020, or if your expectations were unrealistic the first time you did this or for a given group of students. You can simply publish a new version, given enough notice. This is what we did in April, once we realized that we were not going to have the contact time needed to move students higher in the learning progressions on several standards. So we dropped one entire standard and slightly amended the scale used, shifting it down one level. It was an easy fix, and it eliminated all stress associated with school due to a situation completely out of our control.

Development

Let's get into the nitty-gritty! How exactly did we determine these benchmarks and grade translations? We first identified what we wanted our *best* student in that class to be able to do. In general, our best AP student should be able to achieve Expert level in seven of the nine standards because to get a 5 on the AP Physics 1 exam requires mastery of all skills except feedback, engineering design. On the other hand, the best CP student, who doesn't have the pressure or interest in the external exam, should be able to achieve Advanced in three skills (arguing a claim, creating explanations, and problem solving). That's where the focus of that particular class lies; and this is where the teacher tailors the grade translations to the particular group. More on this in the section "Scaling" below.

Let's continue thinking this through, using the CP-level Physics course to illustrate. After identifying where our best student should be able to end the course by the last unit (three Advanced and the rest Proficient), we went through our standards to see how we could get there. There were two things we were looking for: (1) reasonable pacing, with time for assimilation of skills, and (2) the ability to spread the learning out. Would we have time enough to practice enough to master the skills? Would students be overwhelmed with too much to do at once (see Chapter 3 regarding cognitive load theory)? We chose only a few skills for each unit, which provided six or more weeks to assimilate each skill. We found it helpful to make a chart (Figure 7.7) with our seven units in order to plan which skills we would work on and for how long. The circled ones are units in which we moved to new levels. You can see that each unit had a handful.

We counted three Advanced, with the rest at Proficient; we made this our cutoff for our A– in this class. Students who aspire to this level of achievement must be well-rounded, meaning no skills should be assessed at the Developing level or below. Students who earn more Advanced levels would be highly motivated and receive individual instruction on how to move from Proficient to Advanced if and when they are ready to do so.

(A side note: You may be wondering, "Why not have a student be at Expert level to earn an A?" Those students who are able to get to that level in 10 months are in our Honors and AP classes. That's mostly because they come into our class at a higher level—usually able to start unit 1 at

Figure 7.7 Benchmark planning

Course: Conceptual Physics

STANDARD / UNIT	DC CIRCUITS	MAGNETISM	KINEMATICS	NEWTON'S LAWS	ENERGY	MOMENTUM	2D MOTION
Experimental design	B	D (circled)	D	P (circled)	P	P	P
Data analysis	B	D (circled)	D	D	D	P (circled)	P
Arguing a claim	D (circled)	D	P (circled)	P	A (circled)	A	A
Using feedback	B	B	D (circled)	D	D	P (circled)	P
Creating explanations	D (circled)	D	P (circled)	P	A (circled)	A	A
Problem solving	D (circled)	D	P (circled)	P	A (circled)	A	A
Graph interpretation	B	D (circled)	D	D	D	P (circled)	P
Graph creation	B	B	D (circled)	D	P (circled)	P	P
Engineering design cycle	B	D (circled)	D	P (circled)	P	P	P

Note: B–Beginning, D–Developing, P–Proficient, A–Advanced

the Developing level for most skills—and progress more quickly, whether due to previous exposure, innate talent, or internal drive. We do not even introduce Expert-level skills in our CP Physics due to time constraints.)

Once you identify that "ideal student," then you can identify what is the minimum that is acceptable to say that the student passed your class. Is it simply performing at the Beginning level on all nine skills? That's what we determined: students may not have any "Not enough evidence" and must complete the minimum requirements for the course (see Chapter 4) in order to pass this course. We then created a roughly evenly divided scale between those two extremes.

When this design was fully fleshed out, we found that it made sense. And when it makes sense, then it's easy to explain and use. The letter grades and percentages used in traditional grading now had meaning to us. A student who earned a B was one who had proficiency in most categories. *Proficiency* is more than a word; it represents a very specific set of skills.

Scaling the Course

Ideally, the same courses will use the same standards. For example, we have five different physics courses: AP Physics 1, Honors Physics, Physics, Conceptual Physics, and Replacement Physics. All five courses use the same nine standards in the same types of assessments. Most of the assessments themselves are identical, but the pace and breadth of the courses differ. Do you have curricula like that? Or maybe you have English for grades 9, 10, 11, and 12, which have scaffolded or spiraled skills from year to year. Instead of making brand new, unique rubrics for each course, consider that you may be able to use one rubric that spans multiple years and simply adjust what defines mastery at that grade level or in that course!

As an example, compare our AP Physics grade translation with that of the Physics grade translation in Figure 7.2. For a student to earn an A, AP Physics requires mastery of all skills at a high level. If students want to earn a 4 or 5 on the AP exam, they must have all skills at the Advanced level and several at the Expert level (see Figure 7.8). Therefore, the requirements to excel in this class are much more rigorous, which won't come as a surprise. This is baked into most of our courses, traditional or not. We have higher expectations for Honors and AP classes, and we assess students accordingly. What we don't do traditionally is see where this fits into a continuum.

We also thought through what a student going through the motions would earn. Imagine a student in an average-level class, who is just showing up, doing enough work during class to get by but not much more. Those are generally students who earn a C in an average course. But what if a student like that was in an Honors or AP-level class? I know that in AP Physics 1, those barely trying will earn a 1 on the AP exam;

Figure 7.8 AP end of course

At the end of the school year (June), for a student taking AP Physics 1

PROCESS STANDARD SCORE REQUIREMENTS TOTAL OF . . .	MINIMUM REQUIREMENTS	WILL EARN AN END-OF-YEAR COURSE GRADE OF . . .
Any 6 standards at Expert level	With no standard lower than Advanced	A+
Any 3 standards at Expert level	With no standard lower than Advanced	A
Any 9 standards at Advanced level	With no standard lower than Proficient	A–
Any 6 standards at Advanced level	With no standard lower than Proficient	B+
Any 3 standards at Advanced level	With no standard lower than Proficient	B
Any 9 standards at Proficient level	With no standard lower than Developing	B–
Any 6 standards at Proficient level	With no standard lower than Developing	C+
Any 3 standards at Proficient level	With no standard lower than Developing	C
Any 9 standards at Developing level	With no standard lower than Beginning	C–
Any 6 standards at Developing level	With no standard lower than Beginning	D+
Any 3 standards at Developing level	With no standard lower than Beginning	D
Met all minimum course requirements	With no standard lower than Beginning	D–
Not enough evidence to evaluate 1 or more standards		F

Note: AP, Advanced Placement.

that should translate roughly to a grade in the 60s, or a D. This helped shape our lowest levels in the chart above. To get into the C range, AP students must have all nine standards at a minimum of Developing. You can continue this process to scale any course while keeping the standards themselves uniform.

Using for Quarterly or Semester Grades

First, it is extremely important to communicate that these are solely progress reports. They will not get factored into the final grade at all. We use this opportunity to have a conversation about whether or not the current rate of progress puts students on track to meet their goals. As noted in the section "Development" in this chapter, we evaluated the opportunities we were providing to students to practice each skill in every unit we study. When we must translate to a letter grade for the quarter or semester, we refer back to Figure 7.7. We look at the unit that we are in at the time of translation and identify the targeted level of development for that unit, which translates to an A–. We then use a similar approach to the one described earlier to scale the rest of the grades.

Reporting Skills Progress in the Gradebook

There are many different ways to organize your gradebook. While we report the same major categories, we differ slightly in our reporting. When an approach is individual, we note this by changing to the first person.

The most important change we made to the gradebook is removing numerical feedback until we absolutely must have it. In many cases we can customize our reporting tools, substituting with our learning progression language instead of points. We can weight these as 0 points and have this be informative. At the end of unit 2, our gradebooks looked something like Figure 7.9.

Note that each row represents a different student. Each of the nine standards is updated with the most current achievement level for that student. The pins signify comments, such as "At the end of unit 2 (on 11/18) our targeted performance level is Proficient. If you have not attained that level yet (you are at Developing, Beginning, or No Evidence), please come see me for help." This note helps students and parents evaluate if the student is "on track" or not, without having to open up the grade translation chart. There is no number or letter grade associated with this progress report. At the end of the next unit we replace all of the scores with the unit 3 achievement levels and a new note.

Elise

I track student results unit-by-unit using an Excel spreadsheet, which allows me to examine trends, analyze individual and class progress, and determine grades at key points during the year. My LMS allows me to download the most current scores as a CSV file, which I copy into Excel. Figure 7.10 shows a screenshot of the unit 3 page. Note that along the bottom of the page there are tabs for each unit. While in the Genesis gradebook I replace scores at the end of each unit, I keep a permanent record for myself like this.

I should explain that in Excel, I use numbers to represent levels instead of letters or names: Beginning = 1, Developing = 2, and so on. This is for ease of analysis so I can create averages, make graphs, and identify trends. (This is for my information only, and I never share it with students in this format.) As can be seen in the far-right two columns, I compared the unit 3 average with the unit 2 average to get a quantitative snapshot of whether students were improving, plateauing, or regressing and, with this identification, target kids to talk to.

Figure 7.9 Gradebook #1

EXPERIMENTAL DESIGN NO DUE DATE 0.0	PROBLEM SOLVING NO DUE DATE 0.0	DATA ANALYSIS NO DUE DATE 0.0	ARGUING CLAIMS NO DUE DATE 0.0	ENGINEERING DESIGN NO DUE DATE 0.0	USING FEEDBACK NO DUE DATE 0.0	GRAPH INTERPRETATION NO DUE DATE 0.0	GRAPH CREATION NO DUE DATE 0.0	CREATING EXPLANATIONS NO DUE DATE 0.0
Developing	Proficient	Developing	Developing	Beginning	Beginning	Developing	Proficient	Beginning
Proficient	Developing	Developing	Beginning	Developing	Developing	Developing	Developing	Beginning
Developing	Beginning	Developing	Beginning	No Evidence	Developing	Beginning	Developing	Developing
Developing	Proficient	Beginning	Developing	Developing	Beginning	Developing	Developing	Proficient
Beginning	Developing	Developing	Beginning	Beginning	Beginning	Beginning	Beginning	Developing
Developing	Developing	Beginning	Beginning	Beginning	Developing	Developing	Beginning	Developing
Beginning	Developing	Developing	Beginning	Beginning	Developing	Developing	Developing	Developing
Developing	Proficient	Developing	Beginning	Beginning	Developing	Beginning	Developing	Developing
Developing	Proficient	Developing	Developing	Developing	Developing	Beginning	Beginning	Beginning
Proficient	Developing	Developing	Developing	Developing	Developing	Developing	Beginning	Beginning
Beginning	Developing	Developing	Beginning	Beginning	Developing	Beginning	Beginning	Beginning
Proficient	Proficient	Developing	Developing	Developing	Beginning	Developing	Developing	Developing
Developing	Proficient	Developing	Developing	Developing	Developing	Developing	Developing	Beginning
Developing	Developing	Developing	Beginning	Beginning	Developing	Beginning	Developing	Beginning
Beginning	Developing	Developing	Beginning	Beginning	Developing	Developing	Developing	Proficient
No Evidence	No Evidence	Developing	Beginning	Beginning	Developing	Proficient	Developing	No Evidence
Developing	Developing	Beginning	Developing	Developing	Developing	Proficient	Beginning	Developing
Proficient	Proficient	Developing	Beginning	Beginning	Beginning	Developing	Developing	Proficient

Figure 7.10 Excel tracking

CLASS PERIOD	PRO.1 - EXPERIMENTAL DESIGN RESULT	PRO.2 - PROBLEM SOLVING RESULT	PRO.3 - DATA ANALYSIS RESULT	PRO.4 - ARGUING A SCIENTIFIC CLAIM RESULT	PRO.5 - THE ENGINEERING DESIGN CYCLE RESULT	PRO.6A - PROVIDING FEEDBACK RESULT	PRO.6 - USING FEEDBACK RESULT	PRO.7 - GRAPH INTERPRETATION RESULT	PRO.8 - GRAPH CREATION RESULT	PRO.9 - CREATING EXPLANATIONS AND MAKING PREDICTIONS RESULT	UNIT 3 AVERAGE	UNIT 2 AVERAGE	UNIT 1 AVERAGE
	2	3	2	3	3	2	2	3	3	3	2.6	2.2	1.3
3	2	3	2	2	1	2	1	2	3	1	1.9	1.89	0.6
3	3	2	2	1	2	2	1	2	2	1	1.8	1.68	1.5
3	2	1	2	1	0	1	1	1	2	2	1.3	1.23	1.1
3	2	3	1	2	2	2	1	2	2	3	2	2	0
3	1	2	1	1	1	1	2	1	1	2	1.3	1.33	1.4
3	2	2	2	1	1	2	2	2	1	2	1.7	1.67	1.7
3	1	2	1	1	1	2	1	2	2	2	1.5	1.55	0.1
3	2	3	2	1	1	1	2	1	2	2	1.7	1.67	0.7
3	2	3	2	2	2	1	2	1	1	2	1.8	1.78	1.3
3	3	2	2	2	2	2	2	2	1	1	1.9	1.79	1.4
3	1	2	2	1	1	1	0	1	1	1	1.1	1.11	1.3
3	3	3	2	2	2	2	2	2	2	1	2.1	2.01	1.6
3	2	3	2	2	2	2	2	2	2	2	2.1	2.11	1.5
3	2	2	2	1	1	1	1	1	2	1	1.4	1.34	1.3
3	1	2	2	1	1	2	2	2	2	3	1.8	1.88	0.6
3	0	0	2	1	1	3	0	3	2	0	1.2	1.32	1.2
3	2	2	1	2	2	3	2	3	1	2	2	2	1.7
3	3	3	2	1	1	2	1	2	2	3	2	1.9	1.2

The first row (highlighted light green) represents the benchmark that I was aiming for with this class during this unit. The numbers in bold highlight any scores below the benchmark. I could visually identify which standards needed more practice, and I amended our class goals (from the chart in Figure 7.7). In the sample shown, no one in the class was able to achieve Proficient on arguing a claim by the end of unit 3. Therefore, I spent more time in unit 4 on the skills required to achieve Proficiency. In contrast, most students earned Developing on data analysis by the end of unit 3, so I could move them forward to Proficient in unit 4, working one-on-one with the few students still having difficulty. Being able to easily target the strengths and weaknesses of individuals as well as of an entire class makes me a much better teacher. This is why I love this system!

Create and use a tracking method that suits you and your school system best.

Reporting Habits of Scholarship

Like tracking achievement, we report desired habits to suit our own values, courses, and school system. We use the term *habits of scholarship* to describe observable behaviors that can have a great impact on student achievement but should not (or cannot) be directly assessed. Traditionally, this includes things like participation, preparation, punctuality, and coming forward for extra help. We all know that students who participate, come to class prepared, come to class on time, and attend extra help time usually do better overall. Therefore, the purpose of reporting these "habits" is solely to provide information. If a student does not participate, it might explain why the student might not be meeting with success. One method of reporting habits of scholarship is shown in Figure 7.11. If any of these are observed/perceived to potentially negatively affect student growth, they are reported with a U. Any area that is marked as U is discussed during our conferences. There is nothing punitive about this designation. It is meant to be merely a point of discussion.

Elise

I recently began using a different method of tracking assignment completion and participation. As shown in Figure 7.12, I simply kept track of daily participation in video conferencing and submission of assignments. At the end of the week I counted up how many checkmarks the students earned and recorded it. Again, notice that these are worth 0 points. They are just a point of discussion. For example, notice the second row; during weeks 7 and 8 a student didn't show up for any video conferences but handed in all assignments. I contacted guidance and called home to check on this student, who was having trouble managing the shift to remote learning (as so many did). It's purely informative and a way to spot issues and problems before they get out of control. A side benefit is

Figure 7.11   Gradebook #2

PARTICIPATES NO DUE DATE 0.0	PREPARED FOR CLASS NO DUE DATE 0.0	ON TASK NO DUE DATE 0.0	COMPLETES ASSIGNMENTS NO DUE DATE 0.0	PUNCTUAL/ PRESENT NO DUE DATE 0.0	USES EXTRA HELP NO DUE DATE 0.0
					U ♣
U ♣					U ♣
					U ♣
					U ♣
U ♣					
			♣		
					U ♣
U ♣					U ♣

that some kids hate having any imperfections; knowing that you will be recording, regardless of whether or not it counts, is an external motivation to be diligent.

A third method of encouraging good habits might be using a Pass/ Fail system. In the snapshot shown in Figure 7.13, you can see how we tracked content mastery checkpoints, for which students must get 100% before the end of the unit (see Chapter 4 for more details). While the checkpoints themselves are worth 0 points, students need to pass them in order to pass the course. Students struggling to pass these vocabulary quizzes must continue to apply themselves with appropriate coaching.

In this section we have presented several options for reporting "softer" skills in a nonpunitive, communicative manner. It encourages conversation between students, parents, and teachers in order to construct a bridge to success for all students while reinforcing good habits.

Figure 7.12   Gradebook #3

WEEK 6 VIDEO CONFERENCE	WEEK 6 ASSIGNMENTS	WEEK 7 VIDEO CONFERENCE	WEEK 7 ASSIGNMENTS	WEEK 8 VIDEO CONFERENCE	WEEK 8 ASSIGNMENTS
FRI 5/01	*FRI 5/01*	*THU 5/07*	*THU 5/07*	*FRI 5/15*	*FRI 5/15*
5 x0.0	5 x0.0	4 x0.0	4 x0.0	5 x0.0	5 x0.0
5 x0.0	5 x0.0	3 x0.0	2 x0.0	4 x0.0	4 x0.0
5 x0.0	5 x0.0	2 x0.0	2 x0.0	4 x0.0	4 x0.0
5 x0.0	4 x0.0	3 x0.0	3 x0.0	3 x0.0	3 x0.0
5 x0.0	5 x0.0	4 x0.0	4 x0.0	2 x0.0	0 x0.0
5 x0.0	4 x0.0	2 x0.0	0 x0.0	3 x0.0	3 x0.0
4 x0.0	4 x0.0	3 x0.0	3 x0.0	3 x0.0	1 x0.0
3 x0.0	2 x0.0	0 x0.0	0 x0.0	4 x0.0	4 x0.0
4 x0.0	4 x0.0	3 x0.0	1 x0.0	2 x0.0	1 x0.0
5 x0.0	5 x0.0	4 x0.0	3 x0.0	4 x0.0	3 x0.0
5 x0.0	5 x0.0	4 x0.0	4 x0.0	4 x0.0	4 x0.0
3 x0.0	3 x0.0	2 x0.0	1 x0.0	2 x0.0	1 x0.0
5 x0.0	4 x0.0	2 x0.0	2 x0.0	3 x0.0	3 x0.0
5 x0.0	5 x0.0	4 x0.0	3 x0.0	4 x0.0	4 x0.0
5 x0.0	5 x0.0	4 x0.0	4 x0.0	5 x0.0	5 x0.0
4 x0.0	4 x0.0	3 x0.0	3 x0.0	4 x0.0	3 x0.0

Conferencing

Communication is one of the cornerstones of any well-designed learning environment. In many disciplines, one-on-one conferencing is built into the curriculum. For example, language arts and history teachers may sit with a single student while the rest of the class works on an assignment, giving feedback on their essay draft or research paper, guiding them toward the next step in their personal journey. A World Language teacher may have a short dialogue with a student to assess their conversation skills in the language. This, more personalized feedback, is part of conferencing. In our teaching experiences, whether due to our personalities or the curriculum, we never did this unless a student requested it. But now it is an integral part of the class, ensuring that all students have one-on-one time to set goals, discuss progress, and get individual attention.

For formal conferences, students make appointments outside class time three to four times per school year. During this time the student and

Figure 7.13   Gradebook #4

DC CIRCUITS NO DUE DATE 0.0	MAGNETISM NO DUE DATE 0.0	KINEMATICS NO DUE DATE 0.0	NEWTON'S LAWS NO DUE DATE 0.0	ENERGY NO DUE DATE 0.0	MOMENTUM NO DUE DATE 0.0
Pass	Pass	Pass	Pass		
Pass	Pass	Pass	Pass		
Pass	Pass	Pass	Pass		
Pass	Pass	Pass	Pass		
Fail	Pass	Pass	Fail		
Pass	Pass	Pass	Pass		
Pass	Pass	Pass	Pass		
Pass	Pass	Pass	Pass		
Pass	Pass	Pass	Pass		
Pass	Pass	Pass	Pass		
Pass	Pass	Pass	Pass		
Pass	Pass	Pass	Pass		
Pass	Pass	Pass	Pass		
Pass	Pass	Pass	Pass		
Pass	Pass	Pass	Pass		
Pass	Pass	Pass	Pass		
Pass	Pass	Pass	Pass		
Pass	Pass	Pass	Pass		
Pass	Pass	Pass	Pass		
Pass	Pass	Pass	Pass		
Pass	Pass	Pass	Pass		
Pass	Pass	Pass	Pass		

teacher together review the student's portfolio, focusing on their individual goals and rate of progress. As part of these discussions, we jointly revise their goals, provide targeted feedback, highlight areas of strength, and give tips for how to approach areas of opportunity. Each student leaves these formal conferences with an individual action plan to help them achieve their goals.

Informal conferencing is also extremely important to student development. This happens daily during our lessons. As we circulate the room, we're having conversations with students either individually or in small groups. We discuss the targeted level of development at that point in the year and, for the students who need a little more assistance, we ask them guiding questions and provide tips on how to approach a given task or concept. Students who are easily moving through the task will be met with extension questions as we coach them to the next developmental level. In addition to helping us keep students on target for their goals, this approach provides an excellent opportunity to get to know the students personally, which reinforces that we are in this with them. We are their coach in the classroom.

We understand the importance of grades for students. Although we want to minimize the focus on grades, we also want to ensure that their final grade is not a mystery or surprise. Frequent discussions enable students to fully understand what we are trying to accomplish with this method, and they understand that their grade is tied to authentic learning. In addition to the information that is relayed through the rubrics and grade-reporting software, these personal conversations, both formal and informal, have led to improved understanding and outcomes in our courses.

Missing Work and Extra Credit

No discourse about grades can be complete without addressing missing work and extra credit. In the traditional model missing work is given a zero. These zeroes can have huge effects on overall grades and are often used as a battering ram to get students to do work. Extra credit is often provided to "help" students who are struggling, were neglectful, or are grade obsessed. This carrot-and-stick method of grade manipulation means that the end-of-year score is not necessarily correlated with learning and skill acquisition but is more about compliance. This extrinsic motivation—or antimotivation—is actually one of the major obstacles that teachers voice about switching to a gradeless system like this. Initially, I too wondered, "How do I get students to do work if I can't give them a zero when they *don't* do it?" In the gradeless system, every assessment is an opportunity for feedback. Items that are on the list of minimum requirements must be done; everything else is simply practice. If work is handed in late or not at all, the student loses out on practice and personalized, constructive feedback. This means they will not likely improve and achieve their goals. The goals are not ours but theirs. The conversation must revert to putting the ball in their court. And that's all it is: a conversation, over and over again. A student who is missing work is one who doesn't need to be punished but does need to understand the consequences of their actions. They may need support in class and/or at home, and again, only a conversation can help you figure out the answer to that one. What I found, once I wrapped my head around it, is that this wasn't about me. I didn't need to feel badly, get angry, or be upset. The other huge benefit of this approach is that a student who is missing work doesn't have to make up for *everything*, because more practice is coming up, over and over again. This is especially helpful with a student who is absent due to extenuating circumstances out of their control. Since skills are assessed repeatedly, it is easy to simply excuse them from missed assignments, knowing that they will have ample opportunities to practice those same skills in the next unit. There is no need for extra credit either, because achievement isn't tied to accumulating points. Either you have the skills, or you don't.

Concerns and How We Address Them

Especially about parents, and honor roll, and college.

"*Students won't complete work unless you give them points for every assignment.*" We discussed this issue in Chapter 4. It definitely can be a problem because students are rarely taught time management. The funny thing is that students tend to do whatever you pay attention to. We began to simply record the completion of daily assignments. They still didn't count for a grade, but I put a check in my grade log and posted the number of assignments completed each week. The column in the gradebook was weighted exactly 0 points. Students began submitting much more work than they had previously, as described in Chapter 4 and with further evidence in Chapter 8.

"*Parents want to see a grade.*" This requires education. We report progress at the end of each unit. We call any parent who wants an explanation. Most parents are extremely supportive once they understand what you are trying to do.

"*Students won't take assignments seriously if they don't count.*" While there are some students who share this sentiment, our experience has been quite the contrary. Students are often excited to test their ability and take academic risks in a scenario that they know will not negatively affect their grade. It is common for students to take the entire period for a test even though they know that it doesn't count.

"*Administration needs grades for end-of-term (or honor roll, end-of-semester, college transcripts, etc.).*" One way to handle this is to scale the scoring chart so that the trajectory makes sense. Where do you expect the majority of students to be at the beginning of November? That's your B. You'll see on our grade chart that we have a column for the semester (mid-January). We have to report to parents; this grade is simply a progress report, and it does not count. So we scaled down, assuming that if a student has five standards in the Developing level and the other four at the Proficient level, in order to earn a B– at the end of the year, he or she should have at the midyear six standards in the Developing level and all the rest at the Beginning level. This will keep them on the path to successfully earning that B–, as in the next four months, they need to move three standards up to Developing and four up to Proficient. This is very doable.

Our Evidence

Let's preface this chapter by saying that our intention is not to prove the efficacy of standards-based grading. The initial intent of this project was not to publish the data collected but to use them to make meaningful changes in our classrooms. We also thought it might be useful to share data that demonstrate how they inform our practice and enable us to refine our model.

Our method for collecting data was through student surveys, conferences, grade analysis, and teacher observations. Every student had the opportunity to complete the survey; however, they were not required to do so. The surveys were not anonymous, although students were encouraged to answer as honestly as possible and provide as much detail as they could to help us refine the assessment model. We administered these surveys midyear and at the end of the course. For the purposes of this discussion we will only be discussing the results from the end-of-course surveys. The reasoning for this is the varied rate of student development and the fact that final grades for the course are based solely on the final rating in each of our standards.

The survey was composed of Likert scale questions and free-response prompts. The Likert scale rated students' satisfaction with the class, acquisition of content knowledge, problem-solving skills, and lab investigation skills. The free-response prompts were centered on students' strengths and weaknesses, their favorite topic, how they would alter the course, their thoughts about standards-based grading, and its impact on their approach to class, plus a prompt that allowed them to provide any additional information they felt would be helpful. Based on the responses received, it is my assertion that, although the surveys were not anonymous, the students felt comfortable enough with the process and how the survey was framed to provide honest and detailed feedback.

Currently, we have surveyed 378 students of all ability levels, from students with collaborative support to AP-level students, on their experience with our assessment model. These data were collected over the course of five academic years. As discussed in Chapter 4, this model has changed from year to year as we made modifications to address concerns raised by students or issues that arose from our observations, but the focus and intent remained constant. We are aware that this is not a controlled experiment and there are many variables that could potentially be influencing the results. With that said, the feedback we received from students is encouraging us to continue to develop this model.

More than 50% of the students surveyed reported that they saw a significant increase in their problem-solving skills and lab investigation skills, with over 90% of students reporting at least a minor increase in these skills. More than 60% of students reported that they had obtained at least a general understanding of all concepts. Although we do not have data on previous years, this is a stark contrast to the statements we had encountered that precipitated the shift to this model. Before we discuss the results of student satisfaction, it must be noted that the transition to the new assessment model occurred at midyear of the 2015–2016 school year. This is important because a midyear survey was administered to that class as well. Although the sample size is smaller, it does provide some insight into how the class was viewed prior to our transition. Responding to the midyear survey of the 2015–2016 school year, when asked about their experience with the traditional grading model, 10.9% of the 64 students said they did not like coming to class and 23.4% said they enjoyed coming to class. After the transition to the standards-based model, only 4.8% of those same 64 students did not like coming to class, with 33.9% enjoying coming to class. It should be noted that the majority of the students who did not like coming to class after the transition also reported not liking class prior to the transition, although the number of such students decreased. Student satisfaction numbers have remained relatively constant over this five-year trial, with an average of 5.0% of students not liking class, 32.1% of students enjoying class, and the remainder enjoying some aspects of class (11.7%) or being indifferent (51.2%), viewing it as just another class. We will discuss our observations more later in this chapter, but these findings were consistent with what we were seeing from our perspective.

The free responses were coded using a grounded theory approach. All the responses were read and placed in a "bucket" with statements on the same theme. They were assessed as a positive comment, neutral comment, or negative comment. Seven themes emerged: Removing Grades, Motivation/Priority of the Class, Shifting the Focus Away From Grades, Feedback Provided by Teachers, Student Stress Level, Improvement, and Learning.

- Although there were students with strong opinions, both positive and negative, on removing grades, the overall assessment of this was found to be neutral. There were roughly the same number of positive and negative comments, with neutral comments more prevalent than both. The general sentiment was

  Every class does different things and this one is standards, so that's what I do. I think they are fair. We thoroughly go over them.

  The majority of negative comments were centered on the familiarity and comfort of using grades to assess achievement.

- Student motivation and making class a priority skewed to the negative. There were a good number of positive comments about student motivation:

  I gave more effort in class trying to figure out things honestly and giving my best effort constantly even if I struggled catastrophically.

  There were also many students who had the attitude

  I think that whatever you do, you should always go at it with 100% effort.

  They were outnumbered by students who reported that the lack of a number or letter grade made them not care about the class or drop it lower on their list of priorities.

  It can be a bad thing because I am putting more effort and time into the other classes instead of this one.

- Regardless of the positive or negative responses to the removal of grades or level of motivation, the students responded overwhelmingly positively (96% of the students commenting on this subject) about shifting their focus away from grades to learning for the sake of learning.

  Yea, it made me focus on the work instead of the grade if that makes sense. Many students focus on a grade instead of actually learning about the concept that is being taught. But I think this class allows you to focus on learning instead of worrying about a grade.

  I actually enjoy it more than I thought I would. I like the idea that the standards are right in front of you, so you know exactly what is expected. There is no mystery behind it.

  You know what you have to do, and know what you need to improve or work on during the class.

  I didn't realize it at the time, but you are always growing and honing your skill throughout the year.

  I find it easier and more enjoyable to learn. All of my weaknesses have become strengths.

  Although there were some students who reported increased anxiety about not knowing their grade, the majority of students reported that the removal of grades reduced their stress level and allowed them to focus on the learning. They didn't feel the need to be perfect and allowed themselves time to practice a skill and improve.

- The same is true for teacher feedback and improvement in skills and knowledge. Even the students who reported not liking the removal of grades made statements confirming the usefulness of teacher feedback. More than 75% of the students surveyed had positive comments about the nature and method of delivering feedback. More than 90% of the students, including many from the group that disapproved of the removal of grades, made positive comments about their personal development and improvement.

Even though our intent was to shift the student focus away from grades, we understood the importance of grades. To that end, we wanted to make sure that what we were doing was not negatively affecting students' grades. For all of the CP courses we performed a year-end, course average grade analysis for all the years we have taught in this school. As seen in Figure 1, for the three years prior to the shift, Dave's course average was 77.4. There was a slight increase the year we transitioned to the gradeless model and an increase of approximately half a letter grade in the subsequent years to 83.6. Comparing this with Elise's CP course averages, 78.4 for year-end 2013–2015 and 83.2 for year-end 2017–2018, showed a similar increase in course average. When combining all of these students (420 students prior to and 609 after the switch), the course average rose from 77.9 prior to the switch to 83.4 after. The initial instinct might be to dismiss this increase as due to grading easier or allowing students to redo work. However, the opposite is true: the expectations of the course have increased with each year of its implementation. As we improved our approach, it was easier for us to provide targeted support while challenging students to perform at a level that was not previously expected. Also, as noted in previous chapters, retakes do not factor into the student grade. We attribute this shift in average to allowing students to practice and improve without penalizing them. We have witnessed students practicing with more intention, asking questions centered on improvement rather than correctness. Based on our observations, this would be my reasoning for the increase in course average.

In an effort to fully understand what was leading to this change, we expanded the grade analysis. For each year we tracked the percentage of my students who increased their average or decreased their average from the first to the second semester (Figure 8.2). Using half-letter grade as a normal variant in grades from semester to semester, we saw what percentage of students were within that ±5% threshold.

Excluding the students within that normal variant, we then broke that category down into the percentage of students whose average increased by more than 5% and the percentage of students whose average decreased by more than 5% (Figure 8.3). What became clear to me was that there were nearly twice as many students whose average decreased by more than 5% as the students whose average increased by more than 5% in the traditional model. During the 2015–2016 school year, when

Figure 8.1   Graph of year-end averages for 2013–2019

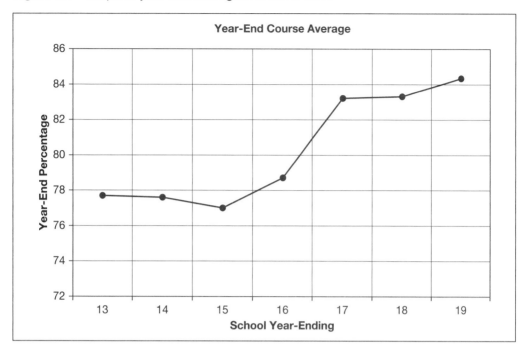

Figure 8.2   Percent change in average from January to June

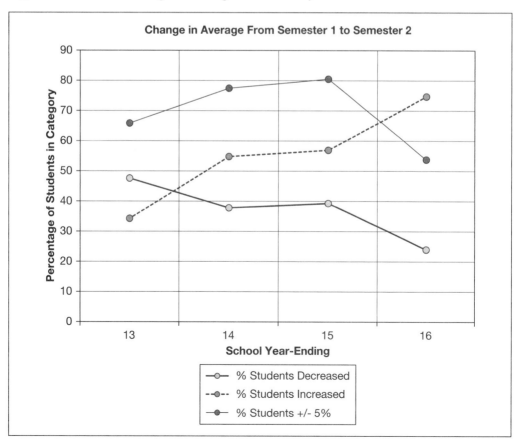

Figure 8.3 Percent change of ±5%

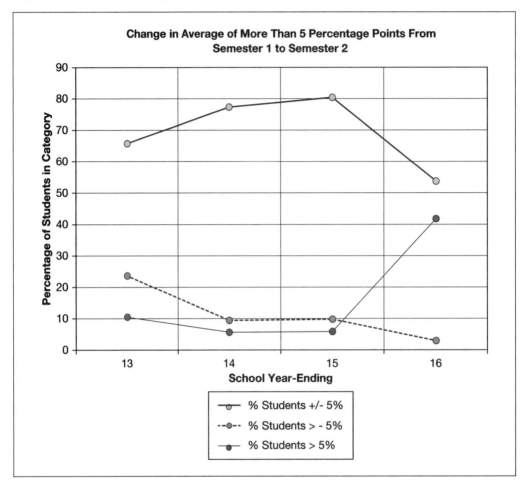

the transition was made, that difference dramatically shifted, with nearly 14 times more students increasing their second-semester average by more than 5% over their first-semester average.

The corresponding shift to skill development and a focus on learning could explain this increase. Students who acquire more skills and knowledge will perform better. The increase could also be in part due to the attitude of striving learners. Part of the reason for the transition to a gradeless model was observing striving learners give up because they didn't see the point in trying. They were resigned to the fact that they would not and could not do well in school. With this model, striving learners revealed their strengths and grew from there. In addition, once student grades are anchored by the accumulation of grades in the first semester, it is extremely difficult to make significant changes to grades in the traditional model. We cannot do any further analysis on this topic due to the manner in which we now track and report progress.

Throughout this process, we have made anecdotal notes and observations. Initially, the model introduced during the transition to standards-based grading was inefficient and difficult to manage. However, it accomplished the goal of shifting the focus away from grades. During that pilot, the positive and negative aspects of this model were almost immediately revealed. The questions students were asking improved. They were more engaged during class time. The stress level was reduced. We were hearing statements like *"You wanted us to focus on learning. I needed to focus on my grade. This lets us do both."* and *"There's no grade, so I don't need to do it."* As we made adjustments to address the negative aspects in future models, student focus continued to shift more toward the development of skills. This in conjunction with a revised unit sequence, meant to support the development of these skills, led to more productive classroom discussions and increased student performance. At that point it became clear that we could assess more with less, which allowed us to spend more time developing skills. Students produced more work of higher quality with less assistance. We also noticed a decrease in parent meetings and more positive interactions with students. Rather than having an adversarial relationship over a grade, we have become coaches in the classroom guiding students through their choices and learning. This has made the classroom more enjoyable for us and seems to have eliminated the negative feelings about the class for most students.

When all of these data are taken into account, we can assert that the implementation of standards-based grading has produced a positive impact on our classes. We have observed a shift in student focus, a decrease in student stress levels, and an increase in student performance. These observations appear to be confirmed by the survey data and grade analysis.

A Step-By-Step Guide to Going Gradeless

CHAPTER
#9

Now that you are thoroughly grounded in all of the pieces that we have used and why, it's your turn to put this together for yourself. We won't beat around the bush: there is a lot of front-loaded work to be done! Once the foundation is firmly established, you will be able to make a seamless transition. Our goal is to provide you with a step-by-step guide to walk you through the process. While you may be tempted to skip the more reflective parts, they are the scaffold on which the more practical aspects are supported, and in our opinion they are essential. Working through these steps will enable you to develop a mastery learning classroom that will radically shift your teaching environment, creating an atmosphere of flexibility, accountability, and collaboration.

We recommend moving forward with deliberate planning and preparation. One goal of this book is to accelerate the learning curve for you, to eliminate the detours that we traveled, as outlined in Chapter 4. We suggest a timeline of 6–12 months to design all of the structural parts, including the behind-the-scenes foundation building. It is beneficial, if at all possible, to find a partner or team with whom to collaborate. The steps in this section are meant to provide general guidance and provoke questions about what you are trying to accomplish with this shift. When background information has been explained in other chapters, we have referenced them, especially for those of you who may be reading the book out of order.

Before working through the following six steps, we suggest having in front of you the following items: your state and national standards, your most common activities/assessments, and graded copies of each assessment (including one each from your best student, an average student, and a student having difficulty in the class).

Step 1: Identifying Your Values

To develop a classroom atmosphere that aligns with your values, you first identify what those values are. Explicitly stating your desired outcomes and comparing the state and national standards with these outcomes is a helpful step in evaluating the design of your course. Looking at what you assess and how the points are determined will reveal if you are communicating these desired outcomes to your students. Note that the outcomes are what you want your students who leave your class to be able to do; these are a reflection of your values or those of the state or national associations that wrote them. (More information is detailed in Chapter 4.)

- ❑ 1a. Before looking at your resources, make a list of *your* values. What do you want your best student to know and be able to do when leaving your class? Be as idealistic and impractical as you wish!

- ❑ 1b. Look at state and national standards. How do they compare with the values in the previous step? Add to or amend your list from 1a.

- ❑ 1c. Using your most common activities/assessments, answer the following:
  - What was the point of each assessment? In other words, what were you trying to find out by having students do it?
  - Are each of your answers reflected in your list of values? If so, make a mark next to the item on the list. If not, add it.
  - Are there items on your list in 1a that have no activities or assessments associated with them? If so, maybe you need to pull out additional work to examine. Or maybe that particular outcome or value is not actually as important to you as you think.

- ❑ 1d. Using the graded copies of your assessments, look at how each question was scored while answering the following:
  - What is the breakdown of points on the assessment?
  - Is partial credit given?
  - How is partial credit determined?

- ❑ 1e. Look for common themes, such as which items earn the most points. High point value indicates "most important." Do these match your value system as stated in 1a?

- ❑ 1f. If necessary, revise your list of desired outcomes to align your values with what you've discovered in 1d. (Or maybe you'll need to adjust your assessments to align with your values, which we will do in Step 5.)

- ❑ 1g. Rewrite your values as "I can" statements from a student's point of view.
  - Use language that a student understands.

- ❑ 1h. We want these to be concrete and observable. For example, if you value "working diligently," as we all do, what would you see? Is there an objective standard of measurement? If not, place these in a separate list called "Habits of Scholarship."

Step 2: Grouping the Standards

To identify and describe your course standards, you will use the list from Step 1, finding common threads. One of the benefits of doing it this way is that you use your own language instead of the more formal curricular wording provided by state and national documents. This step will streamline your outcomes and help you prepare for creating the learning progressions. (More information is detailed in Chapter 4.)

- ❑ 2a. Look for redundancies and similarities within your list.
  - Is the same knowledge/skill assessed by multiple outcomes?
  - Eliminate repetition as needed.
- ❑ 2b. Look for dependencies.
  - Is it necessary to achieve one outcome before another can be met?
  - Draw arrows or reorder to reflect this.
- ❑ 2c. Group all outcomes that are redundant or dependent on another together.
  - Make "buckets" to broadly group related outcomes.
  - Give the "bucket" a name that has a meaning. These are your practices.
  - We recommend limiting yourself to a maximum of 12 practices. Honestly, this is one of those things where the fewer, the better. The state and national standards tend to be repetitive and overlapping. Critically examine your practices to see if you can combine any of them.

Step 3: Creating a Learning Progression

It is useful to look at each practice as a ladder, where each rung is a developmental level and a step toward mastering that skill. The outcomes for your ideal student, as outlined in Step 1 and rearranged into practices in Step 2, are now sequenced to create levels of achievement. The generic framework that we use to guide us through the development is as shown in Figure 9.1.

Feel free to use this in Step 3b, or adapt to your own needs. (More information is detailed in Chapters 4 and 5.)

- ❑ 3a. Place the outcomes within each practice in a logical sequence.
  - Are there prerequisite skills or knowledge that must be demonstrated before students can master the ideal?

Figure 9.1 Language framework

- Not enough evidence: Students did not complete the assignment or address the task in a way that allows us to provide meaningful feedback.

- Beginning: Students try to complete the assigned task.

- Developing: Students use relevant content knowledge to try to address the task. (The content knowledge does not have to be correct, but it must be reasonable.)

- Proficient: Students explicitly and accurately state a relevant concept, but the application is incorrect or incomplete.

- Advanced: Students explicitly and accurately state a relevant concept as well as apply it correctly and completely.

- Expert: Students explicitly and accurately address a complex task that includes multiple steps or concepts.

- What skills or knowledge must be obtained before progressing to the next developmental level?

- A great reference may be your state and national standards. They outline benchmarks for each grade level, which may be helpful when doing this. For example, the Common Core English Language Arts Standards (Common Core State Standards Initiative, 2020) has "Craft and Structure" under "Reading Standards." This begins with kindergarteners recognizing "common types of texts" and moves up through all the grade levels until in grades 11–12, students will be able to "analyze how an author's choices concerning how to structure specific parts of a text contribute to its overall structure and meaning as well as its aesthetic impact."

❑ 3b. For each of these practices:

- What does *trying* (an honest effort to comprehend) look like?

- How can students show that they are providing *relevant* responses, even if they are not correct?

  Within a practice how do you distinguish between understanding and application, as described by Bloom's taxonomy (Chapter 5)? For us, this distinction occurs between the Developing and Proficient levels.

❑ 3c. Determine how many levels you want (or need) to have in order to draw students through to mastery.

- Look over all of the practices, and identify a uniform number of levels using whatever framework suits you best.

- Make names for the levels.
- Drop the skills/knowledge into the levels. You will have to group these; you won't have a level for every distinct prerequisite in your sequence. They will be clustered so that there are several things that must be mastered in order to achieve a level. This means that a student may stay, be "stuck," at Developing while they demonstrate four out of the five applications that you are looking for; they will be on the same level as someone who has yet to demonstrate any of them.

You may find that there is more packed into the higher levels. That is normal! There are more pieces to master at the Advanced level, which correlates to a bigger jump. That is why it will take more time for students to move from Proficient to Advanced than it did to go from Developing to Proficient. In Step 5 you will design the activities and assessments needed to provide students with appropriate support to process and retain this information efficiently.

Step 4: Pairing Assessments and Standards

Now you've created your standards (practices), as well as the learning progressions for each. Although any single practice may be seen in multiple aspects of your coursework, certain assessments pair better with particular standards. When the practices are properly paired with assessments, it makes scoring and reporting them much more efficient. (More information is detailed in Chapter 6.)

- ❏ 4a. What are your categories of regular assessments and activities?
  - To move students through to mastery, you must provide multiple opportunities for engaging with the practice. Because you want to reduce cognitive load, it is useful to keep the types of assessments rather systematic, even repetitive. For example, in our science courses, we were able to group our assessments into three main categories: labs, tests, and projects. This is not to say that we don't do anything else, but these are the assessments that we use to draw students through to mastery.

- ❏ 4b. Which types of assessments or activities naturally fit each practice?
  - You may want to make a chart, something like that shown in Figure 9.2.

Figure 9.2 Aligning standards

	EXPOSITORY ESSAY	RESEARCH PAPER	CLASS DISCUSSION	CREATIVE WRITING	VOCABULARY QUIZ
Practice 1	X				
Practice 2	X				
Practice 3	X			X	
Practice 4				X	
Practice 5		X			X
Practice 6		X			
Practice 7			X		X
Practice 8			X		

- Note that there may be multiple types of assessments that can be used to assess a particular practice. In addition, one type of assessment can be used to assess more than one standard.

- You may want to streamline the process by using only one particular type of assessment for each practice. Just because you *can* assess a skill doesn't mean you have to do so. For example, in our classes, graph interpretation could be assessed on a lab report, but for us it is more effective to assess it on a test. It is a choice, like many things in a teacher's toolbox.

Step 5: Aligning Assessments and Activities

You may find that once you make your chart, there is a lot of repetition and, perhaps, unnecessary work (for you and for the students). This will enable you to redesign and streamline your assignments. The learning progressions encourage the use of formative, low-stakes assessments. These are geared toward narrative feedback to provide students with the information and opportunity necessary to make adjustments to their thought process. It is critically important that teachers are not overwhelmed by constantly scoring and providing long narratives. Therefore, we build in time for student self-assessment. They not only learn how to read and use our rubric but also allow the teacher to provide them with prompt feedback. In this section you will create the lessons and documents needed for class. You may be able to simply make adjustments to the things you already do. (See Chapters 4 and 6 for more examples as well as details on the particulars as noted.)

❑ 5a. Allow ample time for practice.

- Create scaffolded experiences during which you focus on a particular level of a particular practice.

- Not everything assigned has to be assessed.

- Keep cognitive load in mind when designing lessons.

❑ 5b. Create minimum requirements that ensure that students have enough practice and you have enough information to accurately assess them (Chapter 4).

- If a student does not meet these requirements, what is the consequence? Will you provide remediation? What is your responsibility versus the student's responsibility to keep track of this?

- These minimum requirements should be clearly published to students and parents.

- Run them by your administration to make sure that they will back you up.

❑ 5c. Create benchmarks.

- How will you bring students through the learning progression? In what order and pace? As an example, you may want to refer to the chart (Figure 7.7) that we used to design our course.

- Add rubrics to the assessments and activities to communicate focus to the students.

- Limit rubrics to reveal only up through the targeted level of development during the current unit. We literally black out anything to which we don't want to draw students' attention (Chapter 4).

❑ 5d. Provide opportunities for timely, descriptive feedback (Chapter 6).

- Teaching students how to critique their own work is a valuable lesson, especially if we explain what they have to gain, and that there is nothing to lose, by being honest with themselves. We do this on many types of assignments, including labs, weekly checkpoints, and practice sets.

- Peer reviews teach students to provide concrete suggestions, by distinguishing subjective opinion from more objective criticism and by reflecting on what they find useful when receiving annotations from others.

- Conferencing (formal and informal) occurs all of the time, as discussed in Chapter 7.

❑ 5e. Activities should be accessible to all (Chapter 6).

- Differentiation happens in expectations and pacing.

- Basic requirements should allow all to participate (low floor).

- Major assessments should be open-ended enough to provide challenge for those ready for it (high ceiling).

❑ 5f. Assessments should be reflective of practices, referring back to Step 4.

Step 6: Reporting Out

Proactive communication that is easily understood will address many concerns before they are raised. Whether it's fair or not, you need to be more prepared than any other teacher. On initial implementation make sure that all beginning-of-the-year materials (course expectations, requirements, grade translation, etc.) are ready and functional. If your district uses a common LMS, that is a convenient way to organize your course. For districts that do not have an LMS chosen, there are many free versions, such as Canvas, for teachers to use in their individual classrooms, with more and more of them adding supports for standards-based grading. In some cases, districts will allow you to modify your official gradebook. When possible make sure that the gradebook reflects what you are trying to communicate and is easily followed by students and their parents.

We use Canvas as our LMS and organize every unit into modules.

❑ 6a. Use student-friendly language when writing "I can" statements (Chapter 5).

❑ 6b. Language used is specific without being prescriptive (Chapter 5).

❑ 6c. Grade translations (if required) are clearly defined and published at the start of the year (Chapter 7).

❑ 6d. There is a system in place for students and parents to track progress (Chapter 7).

❑ 6e. Other documents you may want to create (for yourself or for students/parents):

- A brief, coherent explanation of what you are doing and why

- *Habits of scholarship:* If you intend to track these, how will you do so? And how are they going to be used in the assessment model?

- *Gradebook setup:* How will you adapt the gradebook to use your practices and communicate your course setup?
- *Communication system:* How do parents reach you, how do students schedule conferencing, when are you available for extra help, and so on?

If you have completed the six steps in the checklist above, you should be proud! This is hard work, and it will not result in perfection. Like all good teaching the tools will have to be responsive to the students and the curriculum in front of you. We continually remind ourselves why we decided to start this journey. It wasn't because it was easier to create but because it produces better results in a more engaging, responsive environment. Remember to have fun experimenting with what works, and most of all be flexible with the system and with yourself. Just like you are creating a learning progression for students, there is a learning progression for teachers as well, bringing you from Beginning to Expert level as you transition to a gradeless classroom. Be kind and patient with yourself, making needed adjustments along the way.

Day-To-Day Implementation

One of the most common questions we encounter is "What does this look like in the classroom?" It may surprise you to know that our class-rooms look quite similar to what they did prior to going gradeless. We still have sequential lessons, do demos, use virtual simulations, perform labs, administer tests and quizzes (which we refer to as checkpoints), and incorporate projects. Yes, we have due dates! In this section we will list our considerations when designing our classroom experience for a given unit. Each unit is roughly seven weeks. If you would like to dive deeper into our rationale, it will be summarized after the list and is detailed throughout the chapters of this book.

Things We Consider When Setting Up
the Day-to-Day Classroom Experience.

- ❏ Do we have a routine?
  - Is there enough repetition to reduce cognitive load?
  - Is there enough variety within this routine to reduce boredom and engage learners in different ways?
- ❏ Do students have sufficient opportunities to practice?
  - Guided by the instructor, either through video or direct instruction
  - Collaboratively, with the ability to get feedback
  - Independently, with the ability to get feedback

❑ What is the most effective way to structure the learning opportunities in order to provide prompt, descriptive feedback?

❑ Are there opportunities to engage with students individually?

Considerations for Content.

❑ How can we use the content as the medium through which all else gets accomplished?

❑ Which activities are a natural fit for the content we are delivering?

❑ What content has low intrinsic load and can be completed independently prior to class?

  • We have students look up definitions for new vocabulary or take notes on a reading or from a prerecorded video lesson.

❑ How can we reinforce these foundational concepts?

  • We use follow-up questions and problems in the form of direct instruction, using apps like Pear Deck or EdPuzzle and completing guided and independent practice sets. Any of these activities allow students to supplement their notes and enhance their understanding.

❑ Do students have the opportunity to check for mastery at the current benchmark?

  • We provide time in class for completing and reviewing independent practice. We do this as a class or individually, guided by the teacher, by a peer, or by self-checking with an answer key.

❑ Is there an opportunity for immediate feedback?

  • In our classes weekly checkpoints are gone over together. Students engage in a discussion about the structure and accuracy of their responses and identify their strengths and areas of opportunity. Again, this can be done as a class or individually, guided by the teacher, by a peer, or by self-checking with an answer key (paper, electronic, or video).

❑ Are we providing students the chance to apply their knowledge?

  • Our unit-long engineering design projects require students to go through an iterative process, reflect on their designs, and apply new knowledge as it is acquired.

Presenting to Students/Parents

Each module is set up in the same fashion. Content is introduced with narrative representations of the concept. In other words, what language do we use to discuss this topic? We then move to pictorial representations, which help students visualize what's happening. This is followed by graphical representations, where students both interpret and create graphs of the phenomena. Finally, we introduce mathematical representations of the concept. This generally requires students to incorporate all the representations plus use equations to solve problems. Within each of these we move from video notes to guided practice, to independent practice, to practice sets. These, along with our weekly lab investigations and checkpoints as well as unit-long design projects, provide sufficient opportunities for descriptive feedback that students can use to progress through the standards.

For classes that need a little more support and direction, we organize this module into daily assignments linked to the home page.

In Conclusion

As detailed earlier in this book, our main focus is to reduce split attention and eliminate redundancies for students, in an effort to open up more working memory to allow learning to happen. Having routines and a systemized, organized landing page will allow students to focus on learning the material, rather than figuring out how to access a lesson or what they should be doing once they do access the lesson. Making sure these complex topics are presented in a way that breaks them down and makes them obtainable to all students will help solidify the foundational understandings on which all other knowledge will be built. Equally important to the organization of the information is how feedback is relayed to students. Providing immediate, descriptive feedback that focuses on how the work can be improved rather than judging a student's ability has proven effective for us. The absence of a grade allows students the freedom to take academic risks, move outside their comfort zone, and challenge themselves without the fear of a lasting negative consequence. Approaching our curriculum from this perspective has led to significant and lasting changes in our classrooms. Our hope is to speed up your learning curve while you implement the changes in your classroom.

This is generally the first time that students have such agency over their grade, but they are initially skeptical. They (like most people) would like to believe that we are *giving* them a grade. But we really are not—they are deciding at what level to perform, whether or not to use the resources, and to strive to improve (or not). Removing the lasting impact of an individual assessment, continually practicing and sustaining long-term effort, incrementally improving over time are all so freeing!

Students need to hear it over and over again, in groups, as a class, and especially as individuals. This is especially powerful in classes populated with striving learners.

In a personal email to Elise at the end of the year, a student encapsulated our intentions perfectly:

> *Honestly, I was kind of scared to do physics last year because people had such a negative view on it and how difficult the class was. However, every time I stepped into your class it was like a new adventure awaited me and solving problems became such a fun challenge. Your class was also one where I could definitely see the improvement from day one to now and further instilled in me that I could do whatever I put my mind to. Whenever I got stuck I felt like I could talk to you and have a conversation about my problem instead of just feeding me the right answers. Thank you for inspiring me.*

Good luck on your journey! We look forward to hearing about all of your successes.

Resources A

Assessing Student Work

In this section we will show how the standards-based rubrics can be used to assess student work. We will look at multiple content areas and grade levels. In some cases we will provide suggestions on how to improve rubrics to clarify expectations for students.

Creating Explanations and Making Predictions

- Not enough evidence: I do not explain my reasoning or make predictions.

- Beginning: I write an explanation or prediction that addresses the reason why I answered the question using information from this unit.

- Developing: I use relevant terminology and/or state relevant Big Ideas in my explanation or prediction.

- Proficient: While making an explanation or prediction, I can correctly choose and overtly state the relevant physics, in the form of definitions, laws, mathematical models, equations, or relationships.

- Advanced: I produce an *accurate* explanation or prediction that fully ties all the relevant physics concepts to the correct answer, in a familiar situation.

- Expert: I produce an accurate explanation or prediction for a complex situation. This may require the use of multiple steps and/or multiple Big Ideas, applying previously learned material where necessary.

Test question for creating explanations: Examine the six circuits to the right, containing identical resistors and power supplies (see Figure AA.1). Assume that each resistor is a light bulb. Rank the bulbs, with the brightest bulb first, and list in order of decreasing brightness. If any are equal, show this with "=".

Figure AA.1   Six circuits (test question)

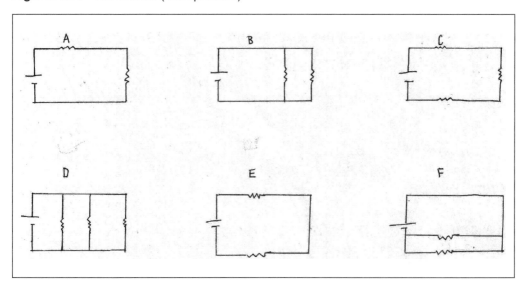

Student sample 1 (Figure AA.2):

Figure AA.2   Student response 1 to the test question

1. Examine the 6 circuits above, containing identical resistors and
   power supplies. Assume that each resistor is a light bulb. Rank
   the bulbs, with the brightest bulb first and list in order of
   decreasing brightness. If any are equal, show this with "=".
   (Pro.9)

   Proof: CIRCUITS A & E ARE EQUAL AND 2nd BRIGHTEST, CIRCUITS B & F
   ARE EQUAL AND ARE THE BRIGHTEST. CIRCUITS D & C ARE IN 3RD
   & 4th PLACE.

   RANKING: B=F>A=E>D>C

This student writes an explanation that addresses the reason why he
answered the question using information from this unit but does not use
any relevant terminology and/or state relevant Big Ideas in the explanation or prediction. Therefore, this answer is a Beginning response (see
Figure AA.3).

Figure AA.3 Beginning

	NOT ENOUGH EVIDENCE	BEGINNING	DEVELOPING	PROFICIENT	ADVANCED	EXPERT
Creating explanations and making predictions	I do not explain my reasoning or make predictions.	I write an explanation or prediction that addresses the reason why I answered the question using information from this unit.	I use relevant terminology and/or state relevant Big Ideas in my explanation or prediction.	While making an explanation or prediction, I can correctly choose and overtly state the relevant physics, in the form of definitions, laws, mathematical models, equations, or relationships.	I produce an accurate explanation or prediction that fully ties all the relevant physics concepts to the correct answer, in a familiar situation.	I produce an accurate explanation or prediction for a complex situation. This may require the use of multiple steps and/ or multiple Big Ideas, applying previously learned material where necessary.

Student sample 2 (Figure AA.4):

Figure AA.4 Student response 2 to the test question

1. Examine the 6 circuits above, containing identical resistors and power supplies. Assume that each resistor is a light bulb. Rank the bulbs, with the brightest bulb first and list in order of decreasing brightness. If any are equal, show this with "=".
(Pro.9)

Proof: Circuits B and F are equal. They are both parallel and have 1 resistor in each branch. Circuit D has an extra resistor so therefore it slows the current down more. Circuit A and E both have two resistors in series. And circuit C has the greatest resistance as it has 3 resistors in series.

RANKING: B=F>D>A=E>C

This student writes an explanation that addresses the reason why he answered the question using relevant terminology, like *resistors*, *circuits*, *current*, and so on. Therefore, this answer is a Developing response (see Figure AA.5). It isn't Proficient because he doesn't define any of these terms, so we can't be sure why the numbers of resistors mattered.

Figure AA.5   Developing

	NOT ENOUGH EVIDENCE	BEGINNING	DEVELOPING	PROFICIENT	ADVANCED	EXPERT
Creating explanations and making predictions	I do not explain my reasoning or make predictions.	I write an explanation or prediction that addresses the reason why I answered the question using information from this unit.	I use relevant terminology and/or state relevant Big Ideas in my explanation or prediction.	While making an explanation or prediction, I can correctly choose and overtly state the relevant physics, in the form of definitions, laws, mathematical models, equations, or relationships.	I produce an accurate explanation or prediction that fully ties all the relevant physics concepts to the correct answer, in a familiar situation.	I produce an accurate explanation or prediction for a complex situation. This may require the use of multiple steps and/ or multiple Big Ideas, applying previously learned material where necessary.

Student sample 3 (Figure AA.6):

Figure AA.6   Student response 3 to the test question

1. Examine the 6 circuits above, containing identical resistors and power supplies. Assume that each resistor is a light bulb. Rank the bulbs, with the brightest bulb first and list in order of decreasing brightness. If any are equal, show this with "=". (Pro.9)

Proof: I chose to rank them this way because power = brightness. In the circuits that are in series, the voltage is being split among the bulbs, making them not have a lot. For the ones in series, they each get equal amounts, making them brighter. The loop rule states that the energy must be dropped off in that loop. The junction rule states that the current leaving the junction must also go back into the junction.

RANKING: D>F>B>E>A>C

Student 3 writes an explanation that not only addresses the reason why she answered the question but also uses relevant terminology (*power, brightness*) and/or states relevant Big Ideas (loop rule, junction rule, etc.). This is a Proficient response because she also correctly chose and overtly stated the relevant physics, by defining the loop and junction rules, even though they are neither stated fully nor tied to the answer well (see Figure AA.7).

Figure AA.7   Proficient

	NOT ENOUGH EVIDENCE	BEGINNING	DEVELOPING	PROFICIENT	ADVANCED	EXPERT
Creating explanations and making predictios	I do not explain my reasoning or make predictions.	I write an explanation or prediction that addresses the reason why I answered the question using information from this unit.	I use relevant terminology and/or state relevant Big Ideas in my explanation or prediction.	While making an explanation or prediction, I can correctly choose and overtly state the relevant physics, in the form of definitions, laws, mathematical models, equations, or relationships.	I produce an accurate explanation or prediction that fully ties all the relevant physics concepts to the correct answer, in a familiar situation.	I produce an accurate explanation or prediction for a complex situation. This may require the use of multiple steps and/or multiple Big Ideas, applying previously learned material where necessary.

Process Standards 2020–2021

U.S. History (adapted from AP Central: https://apcentral.collegeboard.org/)

Elise Burns

Below is a sample response to a document-based question (DBQ) from an eighth-grade class. The task was to identify and discuss two reasons why the South seceded from the Union, using evidence from at least four of the eight documents provided. Using the rubric given in Figure AA.8, we will score this essay.

Abolitionists were people who supported the movement
to end slavery. The North was overflowing with them. The

South however, saw slaves as part of their daily life. Due to this contradiction in beliefs, the two areas were at odds. This contradiction led to hatred, which in turn lead to the start of the Civil War. The Civil War is one of the most famous wars and most studied wars in American history. The Civil War was an argument between the states over slavery. A crowd of eleven southern states left the union in 1860 and 1861 to form a group in order to protect the institution of slavery. However, the true causes of the Civil War were economical and political. Slaves were used to work on the plantations making the slaveowners money, but then President Abraham was elected who was against slave ownership. The South then ultimately rebelled from the states.

Throughout the years of slavery and the Civil War, there were many political issues that arose. Heated discussions about whether slavery was humane or not continued. To start, a huge political problem that arose was the execution of John Brown(Doc4). The reason he was executed by southerners was because he raided a southern military armory, for he wanted to ultimately arm slaves with weapons to fight against their owners. Another political problem that arose was the Republican presidential poster of 1860. This was controversial for the South because President Lincoln did not support slavery. Lincoln wanted to protect the North and its industries. The Republican Party supported anti-slavery, free speech, free territory, and free homes. The North voted for Lincoln because he was against slavery like the northerners and the free states as a whole. The election of 1860 caused many southern states to leave the union. This is because North's antislavery power became more prominent than the South's which threatened their economy that was built of slave work (Doc6). Another big political problem was *Uncle Tom's Cabin*, a book that showed slavery in a very negative way. The author, Harriot Beecher Stowe, wanted to show the evils of slavery, and that's exactly what she did. She believed her words could make a difference, and they did. She influenced many people to believe that this system of slavery was treating humans as property. Many northerners who were not already abolitionists were affected by this book and then, in turn, became abolitionists themselves. The South then realized how many people were now against them leading them to become even more scared of slaves gaining freedom. It was looking like the North and South would never come back together.

There were many economic issues that caused the spark of the Civil War. First off, the South was not an

Figure AA.8 Rubric to evaluate the response to a document-based question

	NOT ENOUGH EVIDENCE	BEGINNING	DEVELOPING	PROFICIENT	ADVANCED	EXPERT
Practice 1: thesis/claim	I do not respond to the prompt.	I respond to the prompt. It may simply be restating or rephrasing the prompt.	I present a thesis that makes a claim that responds to the prompt.	My thesis consists of one or more sentences located in one place, either in the introduction or the conclusion.	The historically defensible claim/thesis establishes a line of reasoning.	The thesis/claim establishes a correct line of reasoning.
Practice 2: Contextualization	I do not elaborate on my thesis.	My response is a phrase or reference related to the prompt.	My response provides a specific historical event to support the claim.	My response relates the topic of the prompt to a relevant historical event, development, or process.	The broader historical event, development, or process is described correctly and in adequate detail. I clearly communicate the relative time frame of the event relative to the question.	My response fully and accurately describes a broader historical context relevant to the prompt, with multiple supporting events.
Practice 3: Evidence from documents	I do not present documentary evidence to support my argument.	I use the content of at least one document to address the topic of the prompt.	My response uses the content of at least three documents to address the topic of the prompt. I may simply quote the content from at least two of the documents.	I accurately describe as well as quote content from at least three of the documents.	I use the content of at least six documents to support an argument in response to the prompt.	My response accurately describes the content from at least six documents. In addition, it uses the content of the documents to support an argument in response to the prompt.

(Continued)

Figure AA.8 (Continued)

	NOT ENOUGH EVIDENCE	BEGINNING	DEVELOPING	PROFICIENT	ADVANCED	EXPERT
Practice 4: Evidence beyond documents	I do not mention any additional pieces of the specific historical evidence (beyond that found in the documents).	I mention one additional piece of historical evidence (beyond that found in the documents).	I mention one additional piece of the specific, relevant historical evidence (beyond that found in the documents).	I fully describe one additional piece of the specific historical evidence (beyond that found in the documents) to support my argument about the prompt.	I correctly use at least one additional piece of the specific historical evidence (beyond that found in the documents or already presented in contextualization) relevant to an argument about the prompt.	I correctly describe and use this additional piece of the specific historical evidence to effectively support my argument about the prompt.
Practice 5: Analysis and reasoning	I do not present evidence to support my argument.	For at least one document, I identify the document's point of view, purpose, historical situation, and/or audience.	For at least three documents, I identify the document's point of view, purpose, historical situation, and/or audience.	For at least three documents, I describe how or why the document's point of view, purpose, historical situation, and/or audience is relevant to an argument.	I use evidence to deepen my explanation, by attempting to corroborate, qualify, or modify an argument that addresses the question.	I demonstrate a complex (and correct) understanding of the historical development that is the focus of the prompt, using evidence to corroborate, qualify, or modify an argument that addresses the question.

industrial area like the North. The South made their living in agriculture growing cotton, rice, sugarcane, and tobacco(Doc1). The slaves were the ones that worked on the farms for free earning their owners of the plantation a lot of money. Free labor. With the election of Abraham Lincoln, the South realized they could lose the right to own slaves, in turn, having to pay people to do the farming. The main reason why the South seceded from the Union was because the North wanted the slaves to be free. The South had to farm because of their location. They needed slaves because the owners could not manage the huge plantations alone, and with the increase in cotton, the demand for slaves went up. In order for the farms to make a living, they needed slaves. Another economic issue that developed was the Protective Tariff(Doc2). The southern states were against the Protective Tariff because it stopped them from purchasing inexpensive products from Europe and made them buy the same items for more money from the North. Although the tariff had changed by the start of the war, the South did not forget the way they were treated by the northern businessmen. The northern economy differed from the South because they mostly relied on industrial manufacturing and sold their products to other countries. Adding on to why the South left the union was John Calhoon who felt that the government shouldn't favor one class over another. The North was more favored than the South because Lincoln became president and the North was where the majority of his votes came from. In conclusion, the war between the states left a mark in U.S. History like no other. It was sparked by many economic and political reasons causing the Civil War which was fought between the North and the South. This war was about slavery, but primarily about economics. Abraham Lincoln wound up being the president to end the era of slavery, ensuring freedom for all.

Evaluating Practice 1: Thesis/Claim

This student has an opening paragraph filled with facts. She restates the fact that "the true causes of the Civil War were economical and political." But she does not present any information that makes a claim about what those were. Perhaps one would look at the next sentence, "Slaves were used to work on the plantations making the slave owners money, but then President Abraham was elected who was against slave ownership," to say that she is talking about economics by mentioning money and political by mentioning the president, but that is unconvincing to me. This would be Beginning level.

Evaluating Practice 2: Contextualization

All of the facts peppered throughout the opening paragraph definitely help provide context for the event, although they are mostly generalizations, with the specific historical event being the Civil War. She also mentions the start but not the relative time frame. This would be Proficient level.

Evaluating Practice 3: Evidence From the Documents

She mentions four documents (1, 2, 4, and 6) but does not quote the content from any. The references are paraphrases or mentions only. This would be Developing level.

Evaluating Practice 4: Evidence Beyond Documents

She doesn't mention any additional pieces of the specific historical evidence (beyond that found in the documents). There is no evidence of mastery for this practice, and therefore, it cannot be scored. This may be intentional on the part of the teacher (and would simply be left blank for this assignment) or may be an oversight by the student that the teacher would want to address for future DBQs.

Evaluating Practice 5: Analysis and Reasoning

This student does not overtly reference the documents. Each document is summarized obliquely, but she doesn't address the document's point of view, purpose, historical situation, and/or audience. Again, this may be intentional on the part of the teacher (and would simply be left blank for this assignment) or may be an oversight by the student that the teacher would want to address for future DBQs.

Why might the teacher not include practice 4 or 5 for this assignment? It really matters what this particular essay was designed to do and when it was assigned. If at the beginning of the year maybe there hadn't been sufficient attention to devote to that skill yet. Or maybe the class was really good at practice 4 and practice 5 already, and this exercise was meant to address some struggles they were having with the first three practices. The system is very flexible.

Let's closely examine an essay assigned by one of our colleagues, Matthew Morone. The assignment is detailed below, with a full student response. After that, the rubric that he used to score this essay is presented, along with why the student earned each score.

Process Standards 2020–2021

English Language Arts: Existentialism Everywhere

Adapted from Matthew Morone, teacher
of English, Pascack Valley High School

You have studied the central concepts and key figures in existentialist thought, discussed Camus's theory of the absurd, read his seminal novel *The Stranger*, and philosophized over the meaning of "The Myth of Sisyphus" and other existential texts and artwork. For this activity you will analyze and interpret the presence of existentialist thought in a contemporary piece.

- Pick a form of contemporary art to study.

- "Experience" it through an existentialist lens, taking note of the existentialist elements within.

- Condense your findings into a two-to-three-page, double-spaced literary analysis paper of your selected piece.

This teacher scored this assignment using a rubric with 6 standards, selected from his 20 that embody practices from reading, writing, speech, and language. Note that he has only five levels as compared with our six. That is fine! Below, you will find a student sample with accompanying scoring using the rubric given in Figure AA.9. We will then compare and contrast scoring with this rubric with that of a different teacher.

Sample Essay: Existentialism Everywhere

Love It If We Made It: An Existential Pop Song

Existentialism is a philosophy that provides two possible outlooks based upon the brevity of life. First, it is important to make the most of the time available since there isn't very much. Second, since there is not enough time to accomplish anything of significance, why bother trying? Existentialism is often referred to as humanism because humans are the only living creatures that know their life span or have a concept of morality. Therefore, this is a style of thinking that is heavily based on trying to address the question: what do you do with your life if you know you are going to die? The song "Love It If We Made It" by The 1975 shows many signs of existential views through the search for meaning, concepts of morality, absurdity and Sisyphean struggles.

Throughout the entirety of the song, the artist talks about the horrible aspects of modern-day life. With lyrics such as "saying controversial things just for the hell of it . . . fuck your feelings . . . Modernity has failed

Figure AA.9 Rubric to evaluate an English language arts essay

	MISSING	BEGINNING	DEVELOPING	PROFICIENT	ADVANCED
Reading: How effectively can you identify and understand Big Ideas within texts and trace their development?	Not enough evidence to accurately assess the skill	The work indicates a beginning understanding of the skill. With help, the student demonstrates partial understanding of the expectation.	The work demonstrates some evidence of understanding, but misconceptions impede understanding. The groundwork for comprehension is evident, but misconceptions prevent the student from understanding the essential question or Big Ideas.	The work shows understanding of the process or content, as well as application in various settings. Some errors may exist but do not impede demonstration of understanding.	The work demonstrates excellent understanding of concepts and content. It demonstrates in-depth inferences, analysis, or synthesis. The student knows the concept of the skill well enough to teach it to someone else.
Reading: How effectively can you recognize and understand how an author's choices (words, structure, etc.) affect the text?	Not enough evidence to accurately assess the skill	The work indicates a beginning understanding of the skill. With help, the student demonstrates partial understanding of the expectation.	The work demonstrates some evidence of understanding, but misconceptions impede understanding. The groundwork for comprehension is evident, but misconceptions prevent the student from understanding the essential question or Big Ideas.	The work shows understanding of the process or content, as well as application in various settings. Some errors may exist but do not impede demonstration of understanding.	The work demonstrates excellent understanding of concepts and content. It demonstrates in-depth inferences, analysis, or synthesis. The student knows the concept of the skill well enough to teach it to someone else.

	MISSING	BEGINNING	DEVELOPING	PROFICIENT	ADVANCED
Reading: How effectively can you draw connections between one text and one or more others?	Not enough evidence to accurately assess the skill	The work indicates a beginning understanding of the skill. With help, the student demonstrates partial understanding of the expectation.	The work demonstrates some evidence of understanding, but misconceptions impede understanding. The groundwork for comprehension is evident, but misconceptions prevent the student from understanding the essential question or Big Ideas.	The work shows understanding of the process or content, as well as application in various settings. Some errors may exist but do not impede demonstration of understanding.	The work demonstrates excellent understanding of concepts and content. It demonstrates in-depth inferences, analysis, or synthesis. The student knows the concept of the skill well enough to teach it to someone else.
Writing: How effectively can you write clearly and succinctly with appropriate tone, diction, and voice?	Not enough evidence to accurately assess the skill	The work indicates a beginning understanding of the skill. With help, the student demonstrates partial understanding of the expectation.	The work demonstrates some evidence of understanding, but misconceptions impede understanding. The groundwork for comprehension is evident, but misconceptions prevent the student from understanding the essential question or Big Ideas.	The work shows understanding of the process or content, as well as application in various settings. Some errors may exist but do not impede demonstration of understanding.	The work demonstrates excellent understanding of concepts and content. It demonstrates in-depth inferences, analysis, or synthesis. The student knows the concept of the skill well enough to teach it to someone else.

(Continued)

	MISSING	BEGINNING	DEVELOPING	PROFICIENT	ADVANCED
Language: How effectively can you demonstrate grade-level mastery of grammar in writing and speech?	Not enough evidence to accurately assess the skill	The work indicates a beginning understanding of the skill. With help, the student demonstrates partial understanding of the expectation.	The work demonstrates some evidence of understanding, but misconceptions impede understanding. The groundwork for comprehension is evident, but misconceptions prevent the student from understanding the essential question or Big Ideas.	The work shows understanding of the process or content, as well as application in various settings. Some errors may exist but do not impede demonstration of understanding.	The work demonstrates excellent understanding of concepts and content. It demonstrates in-depth inferences, analysis, or synthesis. The student knows the concept of the skill well enough to teach it to someone else.
Language: How effectively can you recognize and demonstrate appropriate writing mechanics in your own writing and that of others?	Not enough evidence to accurately assess the skill	The work indicates a beginning understanding of the skill. With help, the student demonstrates partial understanding of the expectation.	The work demonstrates some evidence of understanding, but misconceptions impede understanding. The groundwork for comprehension is evident, but misconceptions prevent the student from understanding the essential question or Big Ideas.	The work shows understanding of the process or content, as well as application in various settings. Some errors may exist but do not impede demonstration of understanding.	The work demonstrates excellent understanding of concepts and content. It demonstrates in-depth inferences, analysis, or synthesis. The student knows the concept of the skill well enough to teach it to someone else.

Source: Mr. Matthew Morone, New Jersey

us . . ." (Genius lines 2,8,11), it is clear the artist is unhappy and is striving to find meaning in a seemingly meaningless world. Throughout the verses and bridge, there is a dump of information in which the artist crams one shocking fact after another. The band gathered newspaper clippings from the entire year and used them to create unfiltered lyrics such as "A beach of drowning three-year-olds . . . The war has been incited and guess what, you're all invited." While talking about the poor political, economic and environmental decisions people and governments have made, the artist is searching for meaning without much success. People seem to make random choices or even worse, no choices, in spite of the fact that tragedies abound. This lack of planning or taking a stand seems to confuse and anger the singer throughout the song. In addition, the artist comments that even though there are supposedly concrete facts, how does one really know what truth is? "Truth is only hearsay. We're just left to decay. Modernity has failed us."(Genius 9-11). The second sentence reveals thoughts of mortality and the short life-span that people have. Leading to the third sentence about the fragility of society and how poorly it takes care of its members.

"The Myth of Sisyphus" as interpreted by Albert Camus, is about a Greek man who gets punished by the gods and is condemned to an unfulfilling life in the underworld. The man, Sisyphus, has to push a rock up a mountain, but as soon as the rock almost reaches the top, it rolls back down. Despite the fact that it's an unforgiving and strenuous task, Sisyphus is willing to do it over and over. Expecting a different outcome when employing the same action is an example of absurdity. Since Sisyphus initially continued to try to get the rock over the crest of the mountain, this is considered absurd. His job is often called a never-ending burden and sparks the existentialist question, what is the meaning? Even though this should seem like a tragedy, Camus would argue that "one must imagine Sisyphus happy" (Camus paragraph 9). He said this because, unlike essentialists, who believe that you are *born* with a purpose, existentialists believe that you *find* your purpose. Therefore, Sisyphus must be happy because he has a purpose. He finds that his purpose is not to push the rock to the top of the mountain, but simply to move the rock. "His fate belongs to him. His rock is his thing" (Camus paragraph 9).

The song has parallels with the myth. Like Sisyphus pushing the rock to the top of the mountain, in "Love It If We Made It" the singer reflects the impossible task of finding a way to fix the world's problems: global warming, death, drugs, and racism. In the song, the impossible never-ending burden seems to be how even though every generation seems to think they are the end, life still continues. Is the never-ending burden to make mistakes and to mess up the world and then try to solve the same problems, generation after generation? The futile and hopeless labor Camus talks about is represented in this song but instead of a man pushing a rock, it is a society trying to fix the problems of an irreversibly-decaying world.

When Camus stated, "no sun without shadow" (Camus paragraph 8), he meant there is no joy without pain. The band also seems to talk about that same thought process when referring to the neverending destruction that people forced onto the world. When singing "I'd love it if we made it" it is almost as if he is hoping that the world will survive, but not really believing it can. In an interview in which the lead singer discussed that lyric, he talked about how the resilience of the human spirit gives him hope. His statement that he is not a nihilist means that he doesn't want the people in our world to die, but finds it hard to visualize any other outcome (Healy Chorus). The hopeful lyrics of the chorus contrasted to the negativity of the bridge are the singer's way of wondering about the pain and joy of our short lives. It is almost like he is wondering if the stupid and horrible things are necessary to create the good.

An interesting opinion by Patrick Galley, states that "existential problems are when you have trouble seeing that your life has value, purpose or meaning" (Quora paragraph 1). He also mentions that when people want to avoid existential questions, they obsess over something. It could be drugs, alcohol, or any addictive behavior. It could also be something socially acceptable, like chasing money or even being a die-hard sports fan. This points to yet another reason why this song is existential. The entire song is littered with references to obsessions and addictions such as drugs ("shooting heroin"), being rebellious ("saying controversial things"), making million-dollar companies ("make a business out of them") (Genius lines 1-3).

The entire point of the song and existentialism is to be shocking and intense. It is to be so honest that you are living and speaking your mind freely. You can choose to see the issues and make a change or choose to ignore them. There can be a lack of meaning in life because of these problems or you can find meaning in them; either way, it is existential. In the end, this song leaves its listeners with more questions than answers: What is the truth? Is the only "truth" that exists fake? What is real?

Works Cited

Camus, Albert. *The Myth of Sisyphus*. Translated by Justin O'Brien, 1942.

Healy, Matthew, editor. "Love It If We Made It Lyrics." *Genius*, genius.com/ The-1975-love-it-if-we-made-it-lyrics. Accessed 9 Jan. 2020.

The 1975 "Love It If We Made It" Official Lyrics and Meaning. Performance by Matthew Healy, November 1, 2018.

The 1975 - Love It If We Made It (Official Video). Screenplay by Matthew Healy, directed by Dirty Hit Lighting, choreographed by Tobias Rylander, October 15, 2018.

Galley, Patrick. "What Are Existential Problems?" *Quora*, www.quora .com/What-are-existential-problems?scrlybrkr=7c6bbf49. Accessed 9 Jan. 2020.

The Student's Score by the English Teacher

On the first three standards (Figure AA.10)—(1) *Reading:* How effectively can you identify and understand "big ideas" within texts and trace their development? (2) *Reading:* How effectively can you recognize and understand how an author's choices (words, structure, etc.) affect the text? (3) *Reading:* How effectively can you draw connections between one text and one or more others?—the student earned Advanced because she demonstrated excellent understanding of the concept of existentialism, with in-depth application of the characteristics to the song. She thoroughly references the artist's words and the effect of particular phrases and the images they provoke. In addition, she references several other sources, most notably Camus. There are neither errors nor significant omissions. While her ideas and understanding are sophisticated, her writing and use of language are peppered with errors. This resulted in lower scores for the remaining standards. On *Writing:* How effectively can you write clearly and succinctly with appropriate tone, diction, and voice? she earned Proficient because although the work shows understanding and application of the process or content in various settings, some errors exist. On *Language:* How effectively can you demonstrate grade-level mastery of grammar in writing and speech? and *Language:* How effectively can you recognize and demonstrate appropriate writing mechanics in your own writing and that of others? she earned Developing due to numerous spelling and grammatical errors. Either she doesn't know the rules of writing or is ignoring them. Regardless, this is a weak point and detracts from her presentation overall. The teacher gets to communicate the strengths and weaknesses of her work, without conflating the various evaluations by giving an overall grade. Imagine just assigning an average numerical score like 3.2 or an 80% for this essay. What does that number communicate as compared with the rubric feedback?

This particular instructor uses the same descriptors for all the practices, without drilling down into specifics. Arguably, while a teacher may have a good idea of what is good evidence of understanding, this doesn't communicate very well to the student the true distinctions between the levels for each standard. An alternative rubric might look like Figure AA.11:

Figure AA.10 Scored rubric for English essay

	MISSING	BEGINNING	DEVELOPING	PROFICIENT	ADVANCED
Reading: How effectively can you identify and understand Big Ideas within texts and trace their development?	Not enough evidence to accurately assess the skill	The work indicates a beginning understanding of the skill. With help, the student demonstrates partial understanding of the expectation.	The work demonstrates some evidence of understanding, but misconceptions impede understanding. The groundwork for comprehension is evident, but misconceptions prevent the student from understanding the essential question or Big Ideas.	The work shows understanding of the process or content, as well as application in various settings. Some errors may exist but do not impede demonstration of understanding.	The work demonstrates excellent understanding of concepts and content. It demonstrates in-depth inferences, analysis, or synthesis. The student knows the concept of the skill well enough to teach it to someone else.
Reading: How effectively can you recognize and understand how an author's choices (words, structure, etc.) affect the text?	Not enough evidence to accurately assess the skill	The work indicates a beginning understanding of the skill. With help, the student demonstrates partial understanding of the expectation.	The work demonstrates some evidence of understanding, but misconceptions impede understanding. The groundwork for comprehension is evident, but misconceptions prevent the student from understanding the essential question or Big Ideas.	The work shows understanding of the process or content, as well as application in various settings. Some errors may exist but do not impede demonstration of understanding.	The work demonstrates excellent understanding of concepts and content. It demonstrates in-depth inferences, analysis, or synthesis. The student knows the concept of the skill well enough to teach it to someone else.

	MISSING	BEGINNING	DEVELOPING	PROFICIENT	ADVANCED
Reading: How effectively can you draw connections between one text and one or more others?	Not enough evidence to accurately assess the skill	The work indicates a beginning understanding of the skill. With help, the student demonstrates partial understanding of the expectation.	The work demonstrates some evidence of understanding, but misconceptions impede understanding. The groundwork for comprehension is evident, but misconceptions prevent the student from understanding the essential question or Big Ideas.	The work shows understanding of the process or content, as well as application in various settings. Some errors may exist but do not impede demonstration of understanding.	The work demonstrates excellent understanding of concepts and content. It demonstrates in-depth inferences, analysis, or synthesis. The student knows the concept of the skill well enough to teach it to someone else.
Writing: How effectively can you write clearly and succinctly with appropriate tone, diction, and voice?	Not enough evidence to accurately assess the skill	The work indicates a beginning understanding of the skill. With help, the student demonstrates partial understanding of the expectation.	The work demonstrates some evidence of understanding, but misconceptions impede understanding. The groundwork for comprehension is evident, but misconceptions prevent the student from understanding the essential question or Big Ideas.	The work shows understanding of the process or content, as well as application in various settings. Some errors may exist but do not impede demonstration of understanding.	The work demonstrates excellent understanding of concepts and content. It demonstrates in-depth inferences, analysis, or synthesis. The student knows the concept of the skill well enough to teach it to someone else.

(Continued)

	MISSING	BEGINNING	DEVELOPING	PROFICIENT	ADVANCED
Language: How effectively can you demonstrate grade-level mastery of grammar in writing and speech?	Not enough evidence to accurately assess the skill	The work indicates a beginning understanding of the skill. With help, the student demonstrates partial understanding of the expectation.	The work demonstrates some evidence of understanding, but misconceptions impede understanding. The groundwork for comprehension is evident, but misconceptions prevent the student from understanding the essential question or Big Ideas.	The work shows understanding of the process or content, as well as application in various settings. Some errors may exist but do not impede demonstration of understanding.	The work demonstrates excellent understanding of concepts and content. It demonstrates in-depth inferences, analysis or synthesis. The student knows the concept of the skill well enough to teach it to someone else.
Language: How effectively can you recognize and demonstrate appropriate writing mechanics in one's own writing and that of others?	Not enough evidence to accurately assess the skill	The work indicates a beginning understanding of the skill. With help, the student demonstrates partial understanding of the expectation.	The work demonstrates some evidence of understanding, but misconceptions impede understanding. The groundwork for comprehension is evident, but misconceptions prevent the student from understanding the essential question or Big Ideas.	The work shows understanding of the process or content, as well as application in various settings. Some errors may exist but do not impede demonstration of understanding.	The work demonstrates excellent understanding of concepts and content. It demonstrates in-depth inferences, analysis, or synthesis. The student knows the concept of the skill well enough to teach it to someone else.

Process Standards
English: High School

Figure AA.11   Revised English Language Arts rubric

	NOT ENOUGH EVIDENCE	BEGINNING	DEVELOPING	PROFICIENT	ADVANCED	EXPERT
Practice 1: Thesis/claim	I do not respond to the prompt, or there is no defensive thesis.	I respond to the prompt but either do not take a position, or the position is vague or must be inferred.	I present a thesis that makes a claim that responds to the prompt.	The thesis clearly takes a position rather than just stating that there are pros/cons. My thesis consists of one or more sentences located in one place.	The claim/thesis establishes a line of reasoning.	The thesis/claim establishes a defensible interpretation or position.
Practice 2: Evidence without documents	I do not present any evidence to support my argument.	I attempt to provide evidence but may only restate my thesis (if present), repeat the information provided, or offer information irrelevant to the prompt.	I provide evidence that is mostly general, and I summarize the evidence but do not explain how the evidence supports my arguments.	I provide some specific, relevant evidence to support all claims in a line of reasoning, and I explain how the evidence relates to my argument. However, no line of reasoning is established, or the line of reasoning is faulty.	I provide specific evidence to support all claims in a line of reasoning, and I consistently explain how some of the evidence supports a line of reasoning. Where appropriate, I explain how at least one literary element or technique in the passage contributes to its meaning.	I consistently explain how the evidence supports a line of reasoning. Where appropriate, I explain how multiple literacy elements or techniques in the passage contribute to its meaning.

(Continued)

Figure AA.11 (Continued)

	NOT ENOUGH EVIDENCE	BEGINNING	DEVELOPING	PROFICIENT	ADVANCED	EXPERT
Practice 3: Evidence from documents	I do not present documentary evidence to support my argument, although I may present my opinion or irrelevant sources.	I use the content of one document to address the topic of the prompt. I may summarize or describe the source.	I use the content of at least two documents to address the topic of the prompt. I present specific details from at least one.	I provide evidence from or reference at least three of the provided sources, presenting specific details. I explain how some of the evidence relates to my argument. There is some evidence that is specific. I make one point well.	The evidence from the three provided sources support all claims in a line of reasoning. I explain how some of the evidence supports my argument; the correct line of reasoning is established. I uniformly offer evidence to support claims. Complex, accurate, and unique explanations all strengthen the argument. I make multiple supporting claims and adequately support them. I explain the connections or progression between my claims, so a line of reasoning is clearly established.	I consistently explain how the evidence supports a line of reasoning. I organize and support an argument as a line of reasoning composed of multiple supporting claims, each with adequate evidence that is clearly explained. Writing has no grammatical and/or mechanical errors that interfere with communication. Commentary integrates all evidence and succeeds in supporting key claims.

	NOT ENOUGH EVIDENCE	BEGINNING	DEVELOPING	PROFICIENT	ADVANCED	EXPERT
Practice 4: Sophistication	Does not meet the criteria for one point	I attempt to contextualize the text, but it consists predominantly of sweeping generalizations.	I mention individual rhetorical choices and/or other arguments. I use a phrase or reference to communicate a complex thought or understanding.	I describe other arguments. I examine individual rhetorical choices by examining the relationships among different choices throughout the passage. I identify complexities in the passage. I use complicated or complex sentences or language when it effectively enhances the analysis. Sophistication of thought or complex understanding is an integral part of my argument.	I demonstrate sophistication of thought or develop a complex literacy argument by illuminating my interpretation through situating it within a broader context and/or accounting for alternative interpretations of the passage.	I demonstrate sophistication of thought or develop a complex literacy argument by identifying and exploring complexities or tensions within the passage or work and/or employing a style that is consistently vivid and persuasive.
Practice 5: Writing mechanics	Does not respond or plagiarizes the work	I have errors that make communication of my ideas impossible.	I use simplistic or inappropriate vocabulary for the audience and task. I have many spelling, capitalization, punctuation, or grammatical errors. There may be frequent sentence errors that interfere with the communication of my ideas.	I demonstrate an emerging vocabulary, with some awareness of the audience and task. The overall work lacks evidence of careful proofreading because I have several spelling, capitalization, punctuation, or grammatical errors. There may be several run-ons, fragments, and/or unclear sentences.	I demonstrate a vocabulary suitable for the audience and task. There are few spelling, capitalization, punctuation, or grammatical errors. I have only minor errors in sentence structure that do not detract from my message.	I demonstrate a sophisticated, rich, and interesting vocabulary suitable for the audience and task. There are no spelling, capitalization, punctuation, or grammatical errors. I use correct and varied sentence structure.

By developing a learning progression for each standard, the student can better understand the meaning of that practice and use it to grow better and improve. Using the same essay, that student would earn Advanced or Expert on the first four of these practices, while earning only a Proficient level on the writing aspect. The level of feedback provided is much clearer and requires less mind reading by the student to figure out what she should do to improve next time.

It is a lot of work to create this type of rubric, but we always keep in mind that the rubric is not only for use by the teacher. If you want students to actually *use* the rubric, you have to design it for them to read, using language that has meaning to them at their grade level.

We are not limited to going gradeless in high school. This is an essay written by a fifth grader for his English class, followed by the rubric and the evaluation.

Important Rules and Violations in Basketball

Basketball is a fun game. there are lots of rules that you need to know before playing. There are also violations that you can get called for in basketball. You will learn those rules and violations in this article.

Rules

In basketball there are many rules. A shooting foul is when you hit the shooter's arm when they're shooting (see Figure AA.12). A charging foul is when the defensive player has a stationed position and the offensive player with the ball charges into the defender. A blocking foul is when the defensive player does not have stationed position and the offensive player with the ball runs into him. A reach in is when the offense has the ball and the player on defense pushes the player than steals the ball. A technical foul is a bad foul. The team that got fouled will get two free throws and get the ball back. A flagrant foul is worse than a technical foul. The team that gets fouled gets two free throws and the ball back. The worst foul in basketball is a flagrant two. It is worse than a technical or a flagrant one. The team that gets fouled gets two free throws and the ball back but the person that commited the foul is ejected out of the game.

Violations

In basketball there are many violations. Traveling is when you take 3 steps without dribbling.

Another one is a double dribble. It is when you stop dribbling then start dribbling again. Another violation is a backcourt violation; it's when you take the ball over half court then bring it back on your side of the court. One more is a three second violation. A three second violation is

Figure AA.12 A shooting foul

Source: Photo by Serge Kutuzov on Unsplash. https://unsplash.com/@serge_k

when the offensive team stands in the box under the basket (also known as the paint) for three seconds without a shot going up. Another one is a defensive three second violation. It is when the defense stands in the paint for three seconds without a shot going up.

Another one is a five second violation when your team is throwing the ball in from out of bounds. They have to do it in five seconds. This one can only be on the offensive team and the player with the ball has to take the ball over half court in eight seconds.

Knowing the rules and violations is very important to know while playing basketball. If you liked this article you should try playing basketball in a league one day!

Process Standards

English: Elementary School

(Adapted from Common Core State Standards for
English Language Arts and Literacy)

The above essay would earn a Proficient on practice 1 because the student has a clear introduction, he groups information using paragraphs and sections, and the essay has an illustration. The illustration is not helpful in explanation, only decorative, so would preclude his moving to Advanced. He has lots of facts, definitions, and details, as well as linking words.

This would earn him Advanced on practice 2, due to his independent work, the task-appropriate writing, and the two-page typed document. It would not be Expert, because he did his revisions with teacher input. He did use technology for his research and photos and published this on a class website used for peer collaboration.

He would earn a Proficient level on practice 3, because he uses vocabulary without defining terms for people who may not know them, and he has made several spelling and grammatical errors. All of his sentences are complete, but they show no variety in sentence structure (not an issue until Expert) (Figure AA.13).

In Chapter 3 we examined a learning progression for a high school mathematics class. We specifically looked at how the problem-solving practice could be assessed in a 10th-grade Algebra 2–Trig class. The first learning progression in the rubric is shown in Figure AA.14.

Let's look at the two mathematics standards graph interpretation and constructing mathematical arguments, using some student work to again explore the feedback we can give when we don't assign numerical grades.

In the problems shown in Figure AA.15 the student was given two graphs, and she had to use the graphs as well as three choices of equations. The teacher wants to be able to assess if the student understands how the graph and the function relate to each other and how fluent the student is with the meaning of both of those. This is described in the row on graph interpretation in Figure AA.14. In her responses to equations 1 and 2, she uses key vocabulary such as *horizontal asymptote* and *holes*. However, she does not explicitly define the relevant vocabulary to explain the features of the graph; this leaves her at the Beginning level for this question. That might be because that's all that the teacher was looking for here, the teacher asked clarifying questions on another part of the test, or the student chose not to elaborate.

Looking at only the answers (Figure AA.15), being correct is not enough if the student doesn't communicate why, proving the depth

Figure AA.13 Elementary English Language Arts rubric

	NOT ENOUGH EVIDENCE	BEGINNING	DEVELOPING	PROFICIENT	ADVANCED	EXPERT
Practice 1: Text types and purposes	I do not respond to the prompt.	I respond to the prompt.	I introduce a topic and group-related information together and may include illustrations/pictures. I develop the topic with facts, definitions, and details. I use linking words and phrases to connect ideas within categories of information. I provide a concluding statement or section.	I introduce a topic clearly and group-related information in paragraphs and sections and include illustrations/pictures that may be useful to aiding comprehension. I develop the topic with facts, definitions, and details. I link ideas within categories of information, using words or phrases. I provide a concluding statement or section related to the information or explanation presented.	I provide a general observation and focus on my introduction. I introduce group-related information logically by including formatting (e.g., headings). Illustrations and/or multimedia are only used to aid comprehension. I develop the topic by including specific information and detailed examples related to the topic. I link ideas across categories of information using clauses (e.g., *in contrast, especially*). I use precise language and domain-specific vocabulary to inform about or explain the topic.	Illustrations and multimedia are overtly described and explained in the narrative to more fully aid comprehension. There are concrete and specific details included that fully and correctly develop the topic.

(Continued)

Figure AA.13 (Continued)

	NOT ENOUGH EVIDENCE	BEGINNING	DEVELOPING	PROFICIENT	ADVANCED	EXPERT
Practice 2: Production of writing	I do not present any evidence to support my argument.	With guidance and support from adults, I focus on a topic, respond to questions and suggestions from peers, and add details to strengthen my writing as needed.	With guidance and support from peers and adults, I focus on a topic and strengthen my writing as needed by revising and editing. I use a variety of digital tools to produce and publish my writing, including in collaborations with peers.	With guidance and support from peers and adults, I produce writing in which the development and organization are appropriate to the task and purpose. With guidance and support from peers and adults, I develop and strengthen my writing as needed by planning, revising, and editing. I use technology, including the internet, to produce and publish my writing as well as to interact and collaborate with others.	I independently produce clear and coherent writing in which the development and organization are appropriate to the task, purpose, and audience. I demonstrate sufficient command of keyboarding skills to type a minimum of two pages in a single sitting.	Independently, I develop and strengthen my writing as needed by rewriting or trying a new approach.

Practice 3: Writing mechanics	NOT ENOUGH EVIDENCE	BEGINNING	DEVELOPING	PROFICIENT	ADVANCED	EXPERT
	I do not respond to the task, or I plagiarize the work.	I have errors that make communication of my ideas impossible.	I use simplistic or inappropriate vocabulary for the audience and task. I have many spelling, capitalization, punctuation, or grammatical errors. There may be frequent sentence errors that interfere with the communication of my ideas. I correctly use plural and abstract nouns, subject-verb agreement, possessives, and spelling for high-frequency words.	I demonstrate an emerging vocabulary with some awareness of the audience and task. The overall work lacks evidence of careful proofreading because I have several spelling, capitalization, punctuation, or grammatical errors. I correctly use relative pronouns, progressive tense, homonyms and complete sentences, as well as capitalization and quotations (where appropriate).	I demonstrate a vocabulary suitable for the audience and task. There are few spelling, capitalization, punctuation or, grammatical errors. I have only minor errors in sentence structure that do not detract from my message. I correctly use conjunctions, perfect tense, commas, and titles of works.	I demonstrate command of the conventions of standard English grammar and usage, capitalization, punctuation, and spelling when writing. I demonstrate a sophisticated, rich, and interesting vocabulary suitable for the audience and task. There are no spelling, capitalization, punctuation, or grammatical errors. I use correct and varied sentence structure.

Figure AA.14 Algebra 2 rubric

	NOT ENOUGH EVIDENCE	BEGINNING	DEVELOPING	PROFICIENT	ADVANCED	EXPERT
Problem solving	I do not attempt to solve problems.	I attempt to solve problems.	I attempt to solve problems using diagrams, equations, and/or variables.	I attempt to solve problems using diagrams, equations, and/or variables, showing the solving steps.	I correctly solve problems using diagrams, equations, and/or variables, showing the solving steps.	I correctly solve complex or multistep problems using diagrams, equations, and/or variables, showing the solving steps.
Graph interpretation	I do not use the graph to answer the question.	I use some features of the graph, such as coordinate pairs or the general relationship/shape, when answering the question.	I interpret the graph, explicitly defining relevant vocabulary to explain the features of the graph.	I develop a function from a trend line to use in answering the question. This may also include overtly identifying the relevant mathematical relationships shown in the graph.	I correctly associate the function with correct mathematical concepts, interpreting the features of the graph in terms of mathematical equations and theories.	I interpret real-world data or functions in an unfamiliar or complex situation, such as periodicity of phenomena.
Constructing mathematical arguments	I do not respond to the question.	I construct an argument.	I construct an argument that states the reasoning behind my response.	I construct an argument that accurately and explicitly states the relevant mathematical equation, procedure, or theory that it is based on.	I construct an effective argument based on an accurately and explicitly stated relevant mathematical equation, procedure, or theory.	I construct an effective argument for an unfamiliar, complex, or multistep process based on an accurately and explicitly stated relevant mathematical equation, procedure, or theory.

Figure AA.15   Problems and student response for graph interpretation

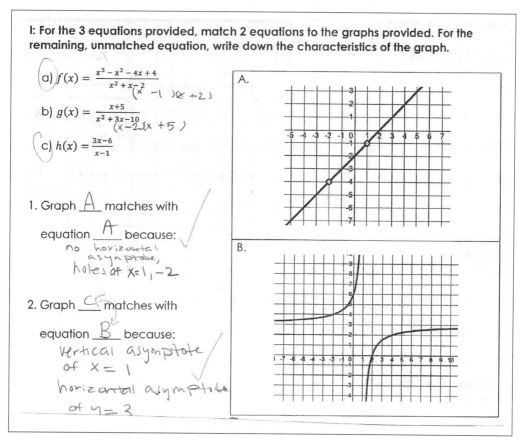

I: For the 3 equations provided, match 2 equations to the graphs provided. For the remaining, unmatched equation, write down the characteristics of the graph.

a) $f(x) = \dfrac{x^3 - x^2 - 4x + 4}{x^2 + x - 2}$ $(x-1)(x+2)$

b) $g(x) = \dfrac{x+5}{x^2 + 3x - 10}$ $(x-2)(x+5)$

c) $h(x) = \dfrac{3x-6}{x-1}$

A.

B.

1. Graph __A__ matches with

  equation __A__ because:
  no horizontal asymptote,
  holes at x=1,-2

2. Graph __C__ matches with

  equation __B__ because:
  vertical asymptote
  of x = 1
  horizontal asymptote
  of y = 3

and/or breadth of her knowledge. But here is where the interesting part of teaching comes in. I would talk to this student and say,

Look at how great you did. Your answers are completely correct. I just need you to provide a little more explanation to get to the next level. Next time, can you define what an asymptote is? Can you explain what a hole is? I just want to know that you know the meaning.

And in this way we coach the student to simply focus on one thing in order to do better next time. Sometimes, it may be appropriate to do a postassessment interview. This is especially useful for struggling students, who may not write with confidence for any number of reasons. If, in discussion, you can ascertain their understanding, you can then give them credit for that and encourage them to write it next time.

For this same class another standard is constructing mathematical arguments (refer to Figure AA.14). Similar to our constructing scientific arguments standard, the learning progression supports the development of responses that are backed up by theory in the form of equations or laws. The three questions in Figure AA.16 are for the same student as above, on a different assessment for the same unit.

Figure AA.16   Problems and student response for constructing mathematical arguments

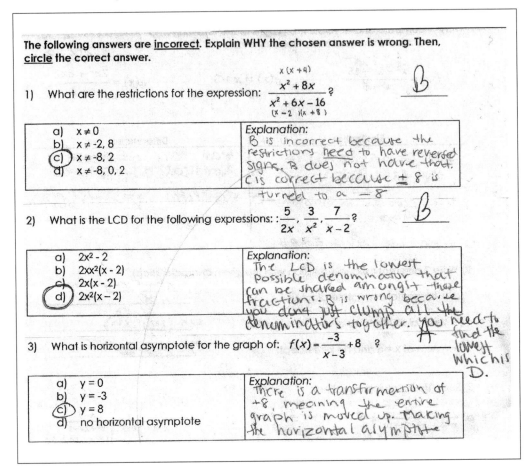

Has she met the requirements for Beginning? Yes, in all three responses she constructs an argument.

Has she met the requirements for Developing? Yes, the argument states the reasoning behind her response.

Has she met the requirements for Proficient? Yes, in each case the argument accurately and explicitly states the relevant mathematical equation or procedure that she used. For example, in #3 she says that "there is a transformation of +8 meaning the entire graph is moved up."

Has she met the requirements for Advanced? Yes, the arguments are effective because they are based on an accurately and explicitly stated procedure or theory. For example, to continue with #3, she says " . . . making the horizontal asymptote shift up 8."

Has she met the requirements for Expert? No, because the teacher did not provide the opportunity to do an unfamiliar, complex, or multistep process. Why would a teacher choose not to allow students to attempt an Expert-level problem? It may not be appropriate for the developmental readiness of this particular class, may not be necessary to demonstrate that level of mastery for this course, or may be too big a leap cognitively at this time of year. For example, in my general education Physics class, we rarely do Expert-level problems because we don't have enough time to practice. Given that they begin in September, students cannot move through the learning progression fast enough to assimilate the skills needed within 10 months. However, an Advanced Placement class will not only be able to do so but is also required to do so by the very nature of the questions on the exam given in May each year.

Resources B

· ·

Student Progress and Setting Benchmarks

With student growth and development as the central theme of our assessment model, it is important to present how the quality of student work improves throughout the year. We will track the progress of a single student through one practice, providing sample work and a rationale for their assessed level of development.

One of our standards is "arguing a scientific claim," which is very similar to what is done in both history and English language arts, in terms of defending a thesis. Specific to a lab, this is what used to be called a conclusion, but it is more concise and structured. It consists of three parts: (1) a claim, (2) evidence, and (3) reasoning (hence the abbreviation *CER*). The standard that we wrote, based on both our experience as well as the Next Generation Science Standards, is worded as given in Figure AB.1.

We thought that it would be useful to examine the progress of a single, typical student's CER over the course of the year. To put it in context, this is work done by a high school junior in a general education class. If physics isn't your thing, don't worry about it; you can still see the change in the responses even if you don't have expertise in the content area.

Unit 1 Lab, 9/26/19

Task: Determine the relationship between voltage and current.

CER: In the lab the data collected represented the relationship between voltage and current (Ohm's law), which states that the current flowing through a circuit is directly proportional to the voltage. This is proven in the data table of the series circuit, because when the voltage (in resistor C) was .058 and increased to 15.21 the current increased as well from .001 to .04. Based on Ohm's law, and my data, voltage is correspondent to current, due to the proportional increase of both the voltage and current.
Sample calculation:

$(R = V/I)$

$R = .058/.001$

$R = 58$ ohms

Figure AB.1   Rubric for arguing a scientific claim

	NOT ENOUGH EVIDENCE	BEGINNING	DEVELOPING	PROFICIENT	ADVANCED	EXPERT
Arguing a scientific claim	I did not write a conclusion.	I write a conclusion.	I present a scientific claim regarding the relationship between the relevant dependent and independent variables, presenting evidence obtained from my investigations as support.	I present a scientific claim that accurately describes the relationship derived from any experimental results, presenting convincing evidence and stating a physics concept, theory, or equation as reasoning.	I effectively present a scientific claim, presenting the most convincing, valid, and reliable evidence obtained from my investigations as support and stating a relevant physics concept, theory, or equation as reasoning.	I effectively tie physics theory correctly, directly, and tightly to the most sophisticated supporting evidence available so that my claim is clearly justified.

Rationale: There is no clear claim (Figure AB.2). She only states that there is a relationship reflected in her data but does not say what it is, followed by the theoretical relationship (which is the reasoning).

Figure AB.2   Scored rubric for unit 1 lab

	NOT ENOUGH EVIDENCE	BEGINNING	DEVELOPING	PROFICIENT	ADVANCED	EXPERT
Arguing a scientific claim	I did not write a conclusion.	I write a conclusion.	I present a scientific claim regarding the relationship between the relevant dependent and independent variables, presenting evidence obtained from my investigations as support.	I present a scientific claim that accurately describes the relationship derived from any experimental results, presenting convincing evidence and stating a physics concept, theory, or equation as reasoning.	I effectively present a scientific claim, presenting the most convincing, valid, and reliable evidence obtained from my investigations as support, and stating a relevant physics concept, theory, or equation as reasoning.	I effectively tie physics theory correctly, directly, and tightly to the most sophisticated supporting evidence available, so that my claim is clearly justified.

Unit 2 Lab, 11/30/19

Task: What is the relationship between the turns per centimeter of wire and the magnitude of the magnetic field strength of an electromagnet?

CER: As the length of the wire decreased, the magnetic field strength decreased as well; this is a direct relationship. For example, in trial one with a wire length of 5.98 cm, the average magnetic field strength was 5.46E−04, whilst when the length of the wire was 2 the magnetic field strength was rapidly lower at an average of 1.83E−3. This represents the permeability of free space because it's the ability of a material to concentrate on magnetic fields (the wire).

Rationale: There is a clear claim (Figure AB.3). She presents evidence in the form of data points, which is generally an unconvincing piece of evidence since it's based only on the two points mentioned instead of an overall trend (e.g., from a graph). *Note:* The first half of the first sentence, the "as S decreased, y decreases" format, is an unsophisticated statement that most students have to be persuaded to leave behind in favor of "X is directly related to Y."

Figure AB.3 Scored rubric for unit 2 lab

	NOT ENOUGH EVIDENCE	BEGINNING	DEVELOPING	PROFICIENT	ADVANCED	EXPERT
Arguing a scientific claim	I did not write a conclusion.	I write a conclusion.	I present a scientific claim regarding the relationship between the relevant dependent and independent variables, presenting evidence obtained from my investigations as support.	I present a scientific claim that accurately describes the relationship derived from any experimental results, presenting convincing evidence and stating a physics concept, theory, or equation as reasoning.	I effectively present a scientific claim, presenting the most convincing, valid, and reliable evidence obtained from my investigations as support and stating a relevant physics concept, theory, or equation as reasoning.	I effectively tie physics theory correctly, directly, and tightly to the most sophisticated supporting evidence available, so that my claim is clearly justified.

Unit 3 Lab, 1/9/20

Lab question: What is the value of acceleration due to the gravity of a sphere when it's tossed vertically, as the ball is moving up, compared with when it is moving down?

CER: When the tennis ball was tossed vertically the acceleration of the ball moving up compared to when it was moving down was inversely related because when the ball was moving up towards its maximum height gravity was pulling downwards on the object with a constant acceleration, thus decreasing velocity, whilst when the ball was at its max height the velocity was zero, and when the ball fell back down the velocity increased (because gravity was pushing downwards). This is shown in my graph because my equation was $y = -10.3X + .92$, and my down acceleration equation was $y = -6.62x + 2.1$. The theoretical equation used was $Vf^2 = Vi^2 + 2a\,\Delta d$.

Rationale: There is an overtly stated claim (Figure AB.4; but using the term *inversely* wrongly). There is evidence cited from the analysis in the form of equations from her graph's trend lines. There is an overtly stated theory, although it is incorrect. It's real physics but does not apply in this case. *Note:* Her claim is verbose and cluttered, with explanations and justifications (which don't belong).

Figure AB.4   Scored rubric for unit 3 lab

	NOT ENOUGH EVIDENCE	BEGINNING	DEVELOPING	PROFICIENT	ADVANCED	EXPERT
Arguing a scientific claim	I did not write a conclusion.	I write a conclusion.	I present a scientific claim regarding the relationship between the relevant dependent and independent variables, presenting evidence obtained from my investigations as support.	I present a scientific claim that accurately describes the relationship derived from any experimental results, presenting convincing evidence and stating a physics concept, theory, or equation as reasoning.	I effectively present a scientific claim, presenting the most convincing, valid, and reliable evidence obtained from my investigations as support and stating a relevant physics concept, theory, or equation as reasoning.	I effectively tie physics theory correctly, directly, and tightly to the most sophisticated supporting evidence available, so that my claim is clearly justified.

Unit 4 Lab, 1/29/20

Lab question: What is the relationship between the mass of a fan cart and its acceleration on a horizontal track?

CER: The relationship between mass and acceleration is inverse because of Newton's Second Law. This is shown in my graph because I have a negative slope of −.0414 which means inverse, and as my mass increased from 531g to 754g my acceleration decreased from .216 m/s^2 to .109m/s^2. In all, Newton's second law states that the acceleration of an object depends directly upon whats inversely the mass of the object, and my equation is a = F/M.

Rationale: There is an overtly stated, correct claim (Figure AB.5). There is some evidence cited from the analysis, pulling the slope of the trend line (instead of presenting the equation of the trend line) as well as the two data points, both of which are insufficiently persuasive. There is an overtly stated, correct theory. *Note:* Here is the first evidence of a streamlined structure. She has a clear claim with no excess words. While her evidence is poor, it gets to the point. Her reasoning is a simple statement of the applicable law.

Figure AB.5 Scored rubric for unit 4 lab

	NOT ENOUGH EVIDENCE	BEGINNING	DEVELOPING	PROFICIENT	ADVANCED	EXPERT
Arguing a scientific claim	I did not write a conclusion.	I write a conclusion.	I present a scientific claim regarding the relationship between the relevant dependent and independent variables, presenting evidence obtained from my investigations as support.	I present a scientific claim that accurately describes the relationship derived from any experimental results, presenting convincing evidence and stating a physics concept, theory, or equation as reasoning.	I effectively present a scientific claim, presenting the most convincing, valid, and reliable evidence obtained from my investigations as support and stating a relevant physics concept, theory, or equation as reasoning.	I effectively tie physics theory correctly, directly, and tightly to the most sophisticated supporting evidence available, so that my claim is clearly justified.

Unit 4 Lab, 2/20/20

Lab question: What is the relationship between the coefficient of kinetic friction between an object and a surface, and the mass of the object being dragged across the surface?

CER: The relationship between the coefficient of friction and mass is that there isn't a relationship. This is shown in our graph because it's a straight horizontal line, and the r^2 value is 0.1597, very far from 1 or −1, conveying that only 15.97% of the data was on the trendline describing our data. This is because of Newton's Second law which says that the acceleration of an object is depends on the net force and the mass of the object.

Rationale: There is an overtly stated, correct claim (Figure AB.6). There is evidence cited from the analysis in the form of the R^2 value from her graph's trend line, but although she states that "it's a straight horizontal line," she doesn't present the equation of the trend line itself (the slope should be close to 0). There is an overtly stated theory, although it is incorrect. It's real physics but does not apply in this case. *Note:* Again, the structure is good; she clearly understands the rhythm and purpose of the CER, even if she is still struggling with understanding the value of the graph and its equation.

Figure AB.6   Scored rubric for unit 4 lab

	NOT ENOUGH EVIDENCE	BEGINNING	DEVELOPING	PROFICIENT	ADVANCED	EXPERT
Arguing a scientific claim	I did not write a conclusion.	I write a conclusion.	I present a scientific claim regarding the relationship between the relevant dependent and independent variables, presenting evidence obtained from my investigations as support.	I present a scientific claim that accurately describes the relationship derived from any experimental results, presenting convincing evidence and stating a physics concept, theory, or equation as reasoning.	I effectively present a scientific claim, presenting the most convincing, valid, and reliable evidence obtained from my investigations as support and stating a relevant physics concept, theory, or equation as reasoning.	I effectively tie physics theory correctly, directly, and tightly to the most sophisticated supporting evidence available, so that my claim is clearly justified.

Unit 5 Lab, 3/11/20

Lab question: What is the relationship between the gravitational energy of a pendulum when at its maximum height and its kinetic energy when at its lowest point?

CER: The relationship between kinetic energy and gravitation energy is direct. This is because the r^2 value is .9498, which is very close to our actual value of 1; also our mathematical model was $k = .7852Ug + .9498$. This is because mechanical energy is being conserved, which results in a constant exchange between kinetic energy and gravitational potential energy, because of the Law of Conservation of energy: energy can't be created or destroyed but it can be transferred.

Rationale: There is a correct, overtly stated claim (Figure AB.7). There is evidence cited from the analysis in the form of the mathematical model developed from her graph plus the correlation coefficient (although she doesn't explain its meaning well.) There is a correct, overtly stated theory, simply presented. *Note:* This is the first time she interprets the graph correctly and presents strong evidence. Because she had been doing well with reasoning for the past few labs, she jumped right over Proficient.

Figure AB.7 Scored rubric for unit 5 lab

	NOT ENOUGH EVIDENCE	BEGINNING	DEVELOPING	PROFICIENT	ADVANCED	EXPERT
Arguing a scientific claim	I did not write a conclusion.	I write a conclusion.	I present a scientific claim regarding the relationship between the relevant dependent and independent variables, presenting evidence obtained from my investigations as support.	I present a scientific claim that accurately describes the relationship derived from the experimental results, presenting convincing evidence and stating a physics concept, theory, or equation as reasoning.	I effectively present a scientific claim, presenting the most convincing, valid, and reliable evidence obtained from my investigations as support and stating relevant physics concept, theory, or equation as reasoning.	I effectively tie physics theory correctly, directly, and tightly to the most sophisticated supporting evidence available, so that my claim is clearly justified.

Unit 6 Lab, 5/29/20

Lab question: Given two colliding cars of varied masses, what is the relationship between the total initial momentum and the total final momentum?

CER: The relationship between the initial total momentum and the final total momentum is given when two colliding cars of different masses are direct. This is shown in my line of best fit because my mathematical model is Total final Momentum = 1.029(total initial momentum. To add, my r^2 value is .982 which is very close to 1, conveying that 98.2% of the data collected was on my trendline. This is shown by the Law of Conservation of Momentum which says that the total momentum of two objects before a collision is equal to the total momentum of two objects post-collision. The Law of Conservation of Momentum is also supported in my lab because my average percent difference was low: at −.1%.

Rationale: There is a correct, overtly stated claim (Figure AB.8). There is evidence cited from the analysis in the form of the mathematical model developed from her graph plus the correlation coefficient (here she explains its meaning well.) There is a correct, overtly stated theory, simply presented, plus support in the form of percent difference to highlight the tie between the theory and the evidence.

Figure AB.8   Scored rubric for unit 6 lab

	NOT ENOUGH EVIDENCE	BEGINNING	DEVELOPING	PROFICIENT	ADVANCED	EXPERT
Arguing a scientific claim	I did not write a conclusion.	I write a conclusion.	I present a scientific claim regarding the relationship between the relevant dependent and independent variables, presenting evidence obtained from my investigations as support.	I present a scientific claim that accurately describes the relationship derived from the experimental results, presenting convincing evidence and stating a physics concept, theory, or equation as reasoning.	I effectively present a scientific claim, presenting the most convincing, valid, and reliable evidence obtained from my investigations as support and stating a relevant physics concept, theory, or equation as reasoning.	I effectively tie physics theory correctly, directly, and tightly to the most sophisticated supporting evidence available, so that my claim is clearly justified.

This progression was repeated by many students this past year, many more than in previous years. Setting unit benchmarks and gradually uncovering the levels made a tremendous difference in the gradual improvement of students over the course of the year. They were able to constantly succeed by taking small steps, and we were able to say, "Yes, you are doing great! Can you stretch just a little bit further next time?" This is an extremely effective learning strategy, especially for students who have pigeonholed themselves as "bad" test takers, not "math people," or perfectionists.

Resources C

Some Full Rubrics

Process Standards 2020–2021

Physics: Elise Burns/David Frangiosa

Figure AC.1 Full Physics rubric

	NOT ENOUGH EVIDENCE	BEGINNING	DEVELOPING	PROFICIENT	ADVANCED	EXPERT
Experimental design	I did not collect and/or present data.	I state the task, collect and present data, and provide description of the procedure followed.	I use the tools and equipment effectively to collect data related to the stated task and organize them into a table. I communicate the methods and materials used during the investigation.	I restate the task as a question that is directly related to the assigned task. I use the available measurement tools correctly. The data collected are complete and can be used to answer the question. The data table is well organized. The methods and materials are descriptive enough for someone else to duplicate the data collection during the experiment. I use a method to reduce experimental uncertainty, which is obvious in my data table.	I ask testable questions that are directly related to the assigned task. I can plan and implement precise and effective data collection strategies and communicate this clearly, succinctly, and with sufficient detail, including pictures. The data table is well constructed, including columns for analysis relevant to the task. I explicitly describe a valid and effective method to reduce experimental uncertainty.	I independently develop an investigation that can produce data to answer an independently generated question.

	NOT ENOUGH EVIDENCE	BEGINNING	DEVELOPING	PROFICIENT	ADVANCED	EXPERT
Problem solving	I do not attempt to solve the problem described.	I attempt to solve the problem.	I attempt to solve scientific problems and show some relevant supporting work.	I solve scientific problems, showing my supporting work so that someone can follow my thought processes. This means that I can show the given variables on a labeled sketch or illustration, diagrams, equations used, and numbers plugged in, and can provide an answer.	I select and apply the correct mathematical process to solve physics problems correctly in a familiar context, including all the given variables and answers, all with correct units. I can use a calculator properly.	When presented with a complex context, I fully apply the problem-solving methodology to independently solve the problem correctly.
Data analysis (in a lab context)	I did not complete my data analysis.	I do some relevant analysis, but it is either very basic or not useful.	I identify multiple sources of experimental error. I choose to do some relevant analyses, such as graphing (creation and/or interpretation), problem solving (calculations), and/or quantitative	I describe multiple, relevant sources of experimental error. I present one or more correct quantitative analyses of the data. I use the available analysis tools correctly.	When correctly describing multiple, relevant sources of experimental error, I offer ways to fit those sources of experimental error next time. I choose all of the most effective analysis	I effectively choose the most effective analysis method for the problem at hand, to identify values, patterns, or relationships in complex contexts. I predict the effects of experimental error on the

(Continued)

Figure AC.1 (Continued)

	NOT ENOUGH EVIDENCE	BEGINNING	DEVELOPING	PROFICIENT	ADVANCED	EXPERT
			error analysis (percent error and/or differently), as instructed, although I may omit one or more significant analyses of the data.		methods for the problem at hand in familiar contexts.	experiment. I offer reasonable and specific suggestions to locate the effects of the sources of experimental error.
Arguing a scientific claim	I did not write a conclusion.	I write a conclusion.	I present a scientific claim regarding the relationship between relevant dependent and independent variables, presenting evidence obtained from my investigations as support.	I present a scientific claim that accurately describes the relationship derived from the experimental results, presenting convincing evidence and stating a physics concept, theory, or equation as reasoning.	I effectively present a scientific claim, presenting the most convincing, valid, and reliable evidence obtained from my investigations as support and stating a relevant physics concept, theory, or equation as reasoning.	I effectively tie physics theory correctly, directly, and tightly to the most sophisticated supporting evidence available, so that my claim is clearly justified.

	NOT ENOUGH EVIDENCE	BEGINNING	DEVELOPING	PROFICIENT	ADVANCED	EXPERT
The engineering design cycle	I do not present any relevant product.	I produce a product that meets the basic criteria.	I document the development of my ideas, communicating the problem, needs, constraints, brainstorming, and any research/background information.	I produce a product that meets all the criteria, clearly documenting the construction of my prototype and highlighting evidence and reasoning leading to at least three iterations.	I can produce a product that effectively solves the problem. I fully document the methodical and iterative steps of the engineering design cycle. I communicate how I made decisions using physics analysis rather than tricking. I choose and present a final prototype design based on my testing results.	I can produce a creative and effective product that meets all the criteria, where efficient use of resources is a driving factor in the design process, documenting my use of all essential steps of the engineering design cycle. Failure inspires further investigation and new solutions.
Using feedback	I did not make changes based on feedback.	I make changes based on feedback.	I identify the changes made, correlated to feedback from my peers or instructor.	I explicitly state why changes were made (or not made) based on the relevant physics or skills requirements.	I make correct and appropriate changes based on the feedback received, or I correctly state why I chose not to do so.	I communicate and document the rationale behind alternate approaches to similar (but not identical) situations, based on the feedback received prior

(Continued)

Figure AC.1 (Continued)

	NOT ENOUGH EVIDENCE	BEGINNING	DEVELOPING	PROFICIENT	ADVANCED	EXPERT
						to the current attempt. I communicate areas of weakness and document the methodical application of strategies that I used to improve.
Graph interpretation	I do not use the graph to answer the question or to analyze experimental results.	I use the feature(s) of a graph (e.g., coordinate pair, slope, graph shape, area, and/ or y-intercept) when answering a question or analyzing experimental results.	I interpret a graph by overtly using relevant features (e.g., coordinate pair, slope, graph shape, area, and/ or y-intercept) when answering a question or analyzing experimental results.	When appropriate, I overtly present a mathematical model and/or the relevant physics relationship shown in the graph. I use this to answer a question or to analyze experimental results.	I correctly associate the mathematical model with correct physics concepts, interpreting the feature of the graph in terms of theoretical physics values.	I interpret mathematical models in an unfamiliar or complex situation, including the use of a coefficient to derive values involving multiple variables or constants.
Graph creation	I do not attempt to create the graph.	I create a graph, and the areas are labeled. This may be a loose sketch, hand plotted on	I create a graph between the relevant independent and dependent	The graph includes all the relevant features, such as a descriptive title, plotted points,	The shape of the trend line, the relationship on which it is based, and any values	I draw a correct graph in a complex situation and/or correctly make predictions of how

	NOT ENOUGH EVIDENCE	BEGINNING	DEVELOPING	PROFICIENT	ADVANCED	EXPERT
		graph paper or made on Excel, depending on the assessment.	variables; areas are labeled with variables and units. I include a trend line for the graph.	and any given or reference values on the axes (to scale) where appropriate. The trend line for the graph is selected based on an overtly stated relationship. (The shape must be in agreement with the stated relationship, although the relationship may be incorrect.)	on the axes are correct and overtly displayed. I include the correct equation of the trend line, with accurate use of slope and y-intercept (or, if nonlinear, the coefficient). With multiple lines or parts there is consistency in scale (values are correct with respect to each other, even without numbers).	changes will affect the graph, using the features of the graph to justify my reasoning.
Creating explanations and making predictions	I do not explain my reasoning or make predictions.	I write an explanation or prediction that addresses the reason why I answered the question using information from this unit.	I use relevant terminology and/or state relevant Big Ideas in my explanation or prediction.	While making an explanation or prediction, I can correctly choose and overtly state the relevant physics, in the form of definitions, laws, mathematical models, equations, or relationships.	I produce an accurate explanation or prediction that fully ties all of the relevant physics concepts to the correct answer, in a familiar situation.	I produce an accurate explanation or prediction for a complex situation. This may require the use of multiple steps and/or multiple Big Ideas, applying previously learned material where necessary.

Process Standards 2020–2021

Algebra 2

David Frangiosa

Figure AC.2 Full Algebra 2 rubric

	NOT ENOUGH EVIDENCE	BEGINNING	DEVELOPING	PROFICIENT	ADVANCED	EXPERT
Word problems	Students did not complete enough assignments or address the task in a way where we can provide meaningful feedback.	I attempt to complete the problem.	I attempt to complete a problem using some type of diagram, equation, and/or variables.	I complete a problem using relevant diagrams, equations, and/ or variables where the reasoning can be followed by the observer showing the solving steps.	I correctly solve a problem using relevant, labeled diagrams and equations, while correctly identifying variables and showing the solving steps.	I correctly solve a multistep/complex problem using relevant, labeled diagrams and equations, while correctly identifying variables and showing the solving steps.
Graph creation	Students did not complete enough assignments or address the task in a way where we can provide meaningful feedback.	I create a graph.	I create a graph using features such as coordinate pairs, slope, and x- and y- intercepts.	I create a graph, explicitly defining the key features used to create the graph.	I create a graph to use in answering a question. This may also include overtly identifying the relevant mathematical features used in creating the graph.	I create a graph given real-world data in an unfamiliar or complex situation.

	NOT ENOUGH EVIDENCE	BEGINNING	DEVELOPING	PROFICIENT	ADVANCED	EXPERT
Graph interpretation	Students did not complete enough assignments or address the task in a way where we can provide meaningful feedback.	I use some features of a graph, such as coordinate pairs or the general relationship/shape, when answering a question.	I interpret a graph, explicitly defining relevant vocabulary to explain the features of the graph.	I develop a function from a trend line to use in answering a question. This may also include overtly identifying the relevant mathematical relationships shown in the graph.	I correctly associate the function with correct mathematical concepts, interpreting the features of the graph in terms of mathematical equations and theories.	I interpret real-world data or functions in an unfamiliar or complex situation, such as periodicity of phenomena.
Constructing mathematical arguments	Students did not complete enough assignments or address the task in a way where we can provide meaningful feedback.	I construct an argument.	I construct an argument that states the reasoning behind my response.	I construct an argument that accurately and explicitly states the relevant mathematical equation, procedure, or theory that it is based on.	I construct an effective argument based on an accurately and explicitly stated relevant mathematical equation, procedure, or theory.	I construct an effective argument for an unfamiliar, complex, or multistep process based on accurately and explicitly stated relevant mathematical equations, procedures, or theories.

(Continued)

Figure AC.2 (Continued)

	NOT ENOUGH EVIDENCE	BEGINNING	DEVELOPING	PROFICIENT	ADVANCED	EXPERT
Drawing connections	Students did not complete enough assignments or address the task in a way where we can provide meaningful feedback.	I construct a connection.	I construct a connection while stating the reasoning behind my connection.	I construct a connection that accurately and explicitly states the relevant mathematical equation, procedure, or theory that is used to construct my connection.	I construct an effective connection based on an accurately and explicitly stated relevant mathematical equation, procedure, or theory.	I construct an effective connection for an unfamiliar, complex, or multistep process based on accurately and explicitly stated relevant mathematical equations, procedures, or theories.
Mathematical modeling	Students did not complete enough assignments or address the task in a way where we can provide meaningful feedback.	I attempt to model a mathematical procedure or theory.	I attempt to model a mathematical procedure or theory using some type of diagram, equation, graph, table, and/or variables.	I model a mathematical procedure or theory using relevant diagrams, graphs, equations, tables, and/or variables, where the reasoning can be followed by the observer showing the mathematical thinking.	I correctly model a mathematical procedure or theory while accurately using relevant, labeled diagrams, equations, graphs, tables, and/or variables to correctly communicate the mathematical thinking.	I correctly model a mathematical procedure or theory for an unfamiliar, complex, or multistep process based on accurately using relevant labeled diagrams, equations, graphs, tables, and/or variables while correctly communicating the mathematical thinking.

	NOT ENOUGH EVIDENCE	BEGINNING	DEVELOPING	PROFICIENT	ADVANCED	EXPERT
Data analysis	Students did not complete enough assignments or address the task in a way where we can provide meaningful feedback.	I do some relevant analysis, but it is either basic or not useful.	I choose to do some relevant analyses, such as graphing (creation and/or interpretation) or problem solving (calculations), for quantitative and/or categorical data.	I present one or more effective methods for quantitative or categorical analysis of the data.	I choose the most effective analysis method for the problem at hand, to identify values, patterns, or relationships for quantitative and/or categorical data.	I choose the most effective analysis method for the problem at hand, to identify values, patterns, or relationships in complex contexts involving quantitative and/or categorical data.

Process Standards 2020–2021

Fine Arts: David Frangiosa/Grace Frangiosa

Figure AC.3 Full Fine Arts rubric

	NOT ENOUGH EVIDENCE	BEGINNING	DEVELOPING	PROFICIENT	ADVANCED	EXPERT
Identifying art elements and applications	I did not attempt.	I can identify a relevant element or application in a work of art.	I can identify and explain a relevant element or application in a work of art.	I can accurately identify and explain an element or application in a work of art.	I can accurately compare and contrast an element or application across multiple works of art, or I can accurately identify and explain multiple elements or applications used in a single work of art.	I can accurately explain how elements and applications are applied across cultures to create specific themes.
Inspiration for visual art work	I did not attempt.	I attempt to visually represent the written word.	I can create a piece of work that literally represents a segment of the written word.	I can create a piece of work that represents the entire written piece.	I use the literary piece to create an analogy in an original work of art.	I use the literary piece to create a metaphor in an original work of art.
Application of art elements and principles	I did not attempt.	I attempt to demonstrate an art element or principle.	I can demonstrate an art element or principle from a given example.	I can demonstrate an art element or principle based on a prompt.	I can select a medium/technique that enhances the demonstration of an art element or principle.	I can accurately explain how the culture, historical period, and medium/technique affect the application of the art element or principle.

	NOT ENOUGH EVIDENCE	BEGINNING	DEVELOPING	PROFICIENT	ADVANCED	EXPERT
Produce an original body of work	I did not attempt.	I have a collection of original work.	My collection of work has a simple unifying theme (i.e., material, color, subject, etc.).	My collection of work has a distinct style.	My collection of work has a distinct style and a deeper meaning.	My collection of work tells a cohesive story.
Organize an exhibit of personal works	I did not attempt.	I have a collection of original work.	My collection of work has a simple unifying theme (i.e., material, color, subject, etc.).	My collection of work has a distinct style.	My collection of work has a distinct style and a deeper meaning.	My collection of work tells a cohesive story.
Analyzing composition principles	I did not attempt.	I can identify a rule of composition/ principle used in a work of art.	I can identify and explain a relevant rule of composition/ principle used in a work of art.	I can accurately identify and explain a rule of composition/ principle used in a work of art.	I can accurately identify and explain multiple rules of composition/ principles used in a work of art.	I can completely and accurately identify and explain all the rules of composition/ principles present in a work of art.
Artistic process	I did not attempt.	I can identify a style used in a work of art.	I can identify and emulate a relevant style used in a work of art.	I can accurately identify and emulate a style used in a work of art.	I can accurately identify and emulate a style used in a work of art to create an original piece of work.	I can accurately identify and emulate a style used in a work of art to create an original body of work.

References

Abeles, V. (Director). (2014). *Beyond measure* [Film]. Reel Link Films.

Abeles, V., & Congdon, J. (Directors). (2010). *Race to nowhere* [Film]. Reel Link Films.

Black, P., & Wiliam, D. (2010). Inside the black box: Raising standards through classroom assessment. *Phi Delta Kappan, 92*(1), 81–90. https://doi.org/10.1177%2F003172171 009200119

Bloom, B. S. (1956). *Taxonomy of educational objectives: Handbook 1. Cognitive Domain.* David McKay.

Boaler, J. (2020). *Aligning assessment to brain science.* https://www.youcubed.org/wp-content/uploads/2017/05/Aligning-Assessment-with-Brain-Science-no-ppt.pdf

Boaler, J., & Dweck, C. S. (2016). *Mathematical mindsets: Unleashing students' potential through creative math, inspiring messages and innovative teaching* (1st ed.). Jossey-Bass.

Brown, B. (2012). *Daring greatly: How the courage to be vulnerable transforms the way we live, love, parent, and lead.* Gotham Books.

Butler, R. (1987). Task-involving and ego-involving properties of evaluation: Effects of different feedback conditions on motivational perceptions, interest, and performance. *Journal of Educational Psychology, 79*(4), 474–482. https://doi.org/10.1037/0022-0663.79.4.474

Common Core State Standards Initiative. (2020). English Language Arts Standards. *Corestandards.org.* http://www.corestandards.org/ELA-Literacy/

Frankin, A., Buckmiller, T., & Kruse, J. (2016). Vocal and vehement: Understanding parents' aversion to standards-based grading. *International Journal of Social Science Studies, 4*(11), 19–29. https://doi.org/10.11114/ijsss.v4i11.1923

Hattie, J., & Timperley, H. (2007). The power of feedback. *Review of Educational Research, 77*(1), 81–112.

Khan, S. (2020, August 13). I started Khan Academy. We can still avoid an education catastrophe. *New York Times.* https://www.nytimes.com/2020/08/13/opinion/coronavirus-school-digital.html

Kohn, A. (2007, January/February). *Rethinking homework.* https://www.alfiekohn.org/article/rethinking-homework/

Lipnevich, A. A., & Smith, J. K. (2008). *Response to assessment feedback: The effects of grades, praise, and source of information* (ETS Research Report Series RR-08-30). Educational Testing Service. https://www.ets.org/Media/Research/pdf/RR-08-30.pdf

National Science Teaching Association. (2020). *NGSS hub.* Ngss.Nsta.org. https://ngss.nsta.org/Default.aspx

Sweller, J. (1994). Cognitive load theory, learning difficulty, and instructional design. *Learning and Instruction, 4*(4), 295–312.

Index

CORWIN

A SAGE Publishing Company

Helping educators make the greatest impact

CORWIN HAS ONE MISSION: to enhance education through intentional professional learning.

We build long-term relationships with our authors, educators, clients, and associations who partner with us to develop and continuously improve the best evidence-based practices that establish and support lifelong learning.